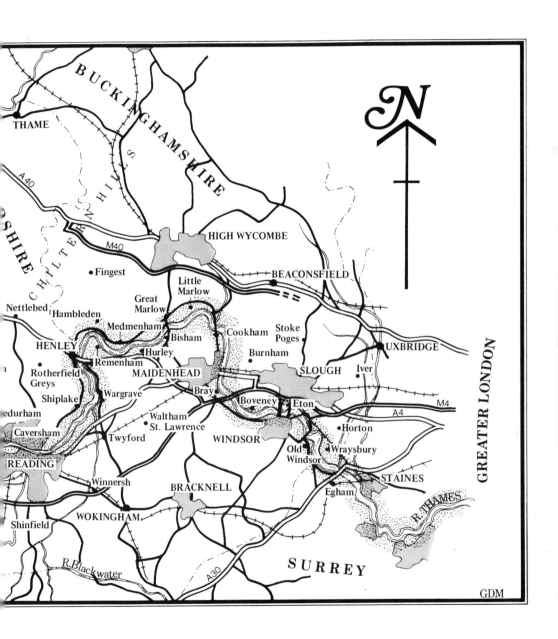

HISTORIC CHURCHES

of

THE THAMES VALLEY

12th Century Lead Font, Dorchester Abbey.

Historic Churches

of

THE THAMES VALLEY

by

GRAHAM MARTIN

SPURBOOKS LIMITED

HISTORIC CHURCHES

of THE THAMES VALLEY

© GRAHAM MARTIN 1973

Published by

SPURBOOKS LTD.

1 Station Road,
Bourne End,
Buckinghamshire.

SBN 0 902875 41 8

Printed in Great Britain by Compton Printing Ltd.
London and Aylesbury.

Contents

ILLUSTRATIONS

ACKNOWLEDGEMENTS

I am greatly indebted to the clergy for their ready co-operation in what must have seemed a nebulous project; for their advice, their precious time, and especially for permission to photograph the interiors, the furnishings and the memorials of their churches.

To my very good friend, Tim Lucas, I am particularly grateful for he has once again provided transport and ably assisted with the photography. On the many fascinating but hectic days we hurtled from place to place, collecting keys, keeping appointments, frantically photographing, and endeavouring to appreciate all that we saw, his personal interest and companionship was a wonderful support.

In the intensive work this project has demanded at home, my wife has borne with immeasurable patience my withdrawal from the family circle, performed countless clerical and secretarial labours and been a willing, albeit captive, critic during the book's gestation.

This acknowledgement would not be complete without recording my debt to the many researchers, of book and guide alike, on whose past labours so much of this work depends.

BIBLIOGRAPHY

Anglo-Saxon England c. 550-1087. (The Oxford History of England) by Sir Frank Stenton, 3rd edition, Oxford-Clarendon Press.

Historic Buildings, The Architecture of the Thames Valley. W. Collier. Spurbooks. 1973

Chiltern Churches by Graham Martin. Spurbooks, 1972

Collins guide to English Parish Churches, edited by John Betjeman. Collins, 1958

Companion into Berkshire by R. P. Beckinsale. Spurbooks.

Companion into Buckinghamshire by Maxwell Fraser. Spurbooks.

English Churches, by Basil Clarke & John Betjeman. Vista, 1964.

English Parish Churches, by Graham Hutton & Edwin Smith. Thames & Hudson, 1957 edt.

From Domesday Book to Magna Carta 1087-1216 by A. L. Poole. 2nd edt., 1955. Oxford-Clarendon Press. (Oxford History of England).

Landscape with Churches by G. M. Durant. Museum Press Ltd., 1965.

The Buildings of England; Berkshire, by Nikolaus Pevsner. Penguin-1966.

The Buildings of England; Buckinghamshire, by Nikolaus Pevsner. Penguin-1960.

The Buildings of England; Surrey, by Ian Nairn & Nikolaus Pevsner. Penguin-1962.

The King's England – Berkshire by Arthur Mee – Hodder & Stoughton.

The King's England – Buckinghamshire by Arthur Mee – Hodder & Stoughton.

The King's England Oxfordshire by Arthur Mee – Hodder & Stoughton.

The Upper Thames by J. R. L. Anderson – Eyre & Spottiswood, 1970.

INTRODUCTION

When visiting the churches of the Chiltern Hills some years ago, one came inevitably to the River Thames where hill and valley meet around Henley, Hambleden, Medmenham and Marlow. Now the opportunity has arisen to revisit these places, each lovely in name and nature, this time in the context of an area which has been a veritable cradle to our English civilization – the Thames Valley.

Here, our greatest river has been both a dividing and a unifying force; a boundary between Saxon kingdoms, and a trade route throughout the medieval age and after. Earlier still, wandering peoples found security in its defensive windings, food in its waters, meadows and woodlands, flints in its gravel banks. Later, roads crossed the river, which was itself a great highway and thus a catalyst between peoples, between ideas. Not surprisingly, settlements were numerous, some developing into towns, other remaining as hamlets.

It was not long before Christian missionaries brought the news of the Gospel; in the centuries since then their churches have grown, reflecting in embellishment or dereliction the ever changing, diverse society which they served – and serve still – as this study endeavours to reveal. It attempts to unravel some of this early history, and concentrates on the Saxon and Norman periods in which were founded the buildings that have become a fundamental part of our culture, witnessing as they do the eternal thread of life in man.

The area covered in this survey – and loosely named the Thames Valley – is the immediate territory bounding the river between Staines and Oxford. This is really the middle Thames for above Oxford the character of the river and scenery changes, and there are no major settlements; while below Staines is London, whose fascinating and complex development requires separate study and where much early history in stones has been destroyed; below London, fords and bridges cease and the river becomes estuarial.

Within this definition, almost all the churches whose parishes are bounded by the Thames have been included, even though in some instances the church itself may be a mile or so away from the river. All belong to the Church of England, the continuation of the medieval Church to which these buildings owe their foundation.

In studying each church much reliance has been placed on published works on ecclesiastical architecture and history. As far as possible this evidence has been checked during visits and is supported by new photography. Also this work builds on the primary knowledge covered in the author's 'Chiltern Churches' so allowing other facets of church history and building to be covered. It is not possible in a comparative study of this kind to include all the information available, nor all the illustrations that the subject merits; but it is hoped that there is sufficient both to satisfy the general reader and arouse the student.

CHAPTER I

Church History

In the area being considered there were many Roman and Romano-British settlements; a few people would have been Christians, at times worshipping secretly, otherwise openly, though in private houses. Churches were very few indeed.

In about 400 A.D. the Saxon invasions began, bringing Germanic pagan beliefs to combine with the ancient native ones. The efforts of the Celtic Christian churches, frail in themselves, only touched the fringes of this mid-Thames area. So Bede recorded that Birinus, who had intended preaching in the remoter parts of England, remained in the south to combat the strong paganism of the Gevissae. They were a tribe of West Saxons centred on Bensington, now Benson.

Birinus, an independent missionary, came in 634 A.D. on the advice of Pope Honorius I. The following year he baptised Cynegils, King of Wessex, whose authority extended over Berkshire, Hampshire and parts of the counties to the west.

The Thames Valley was always an area of dispute with the kingdom of Mercia to the north. At this time Wessex held the north bank, and so it was that Birinus was given Dorchester-on-Thames as his episcopal seat by the King, whose baptism reputedly took place in the river Thame, hard by the present church. Birinus was consecrated bishop by Asterius, Archbishop of Milan. Undoubtedly many other baptisms followed the royal conversion, but Cenwalh, who succeeded Cynegils, was not baptised until about 646 A.D. Birinus had died four years earlier, and although his followers would have continued the work, it would have been limited until the appointment in 648 A.D. of a new bishop, Agilbert, a Frank with contacts in the Celtic Church. He abandoned Dorchester and returned to France about 663 A.D. when a Saxon bishop was appointed, based on Winchester, then the main capital of Wessex. Christianity, through its own good news and through social and political expediency, became the dominant religion

13

in the country, but pagan practices continued in secret causing Archbishop Theodore to prescribe penances for those who resorted to them.

The missionaries' influence was consolidated by the establishment of monastic communities. Thus the first abbey at Abingdon was founded in 675 A.D.

In the early 680's Aetla was bishop only for a short time; this may have been due to the Mercians who over-ran the area around Dorchester at that period. From about 725 A.D. they dominated the whole of Wessex, until the end of the century. Aethalbald, King of Mercia, gave a monastery at Cookham, in Berkshire, to the Archbishop of Canterbury. Aethalbald was also protector of the abbey at Abingdon. His successor was the great King Offa, who, in 779 A.D. at Bensington, defeated Cynewulf, King of Wessex, who was attempting to recover former territories. Mercia retained control of both sides of the Thames until about 850 A.D.; not long afterwards the three kingdoms of Mercia, Wessex and East Anglia were united under Alfred. This was short-lived because the Danish raids on Wessex began in 870 A.D.

The previous year, because of earlier Danish attacks further north, the Bishop of Leicester moved his seat to Dorchester. After the conversion of the Danes the bishop's territory extended from the Thames northward, through Leicestershire, and over the whole of Lincolnshire. In 878 A.D. Guthrum the Dane was baptised, Alfred being his godfather. The Thames was agreed as a boundary, Guthrum occupying Mercia and East Anglia. About this time Alfred fortified Wallingford, as it was a major crossing point, and possibly Oxford, up till then a place of little note. Danish raiders came up above London in 894-5 A.D.; after this hostilities ceased.

In 909 A.D. the Winchester diocese was sub-divided into Winchester, Sherborne, Wells, Crediton and Ramsbury. The last covered Berkshire, and the Bishop had five manors including one at Sonning.

There were new Danish raids in 1006 through Hampshire and Berkshire to Reading, on to Wallingford, then south to Avebury and Winchester. A further invasion in 1009 resulted in the burning of Oxford early the following year. Continuing pressure from the Danes brought about the capture of Oxford in 1013 by which time Sweyn, the Danish leader, had temporarily gained control of the whole kingdom. This was consolidated by Cnut between 1015 and 1017.

The then Bishop of Dorchester was Eadnoth whose territory, it will be recalled, stretched northward to include Lincolnshire. His successors continued at Dorchester until the Norman, Remigius, who was the first bishop appointed under William I following Wulfig's death in 1067. Remigius moved the episcopal seat to Lincoln between 1072 and 1077. Thus the bishopric of Dorchester came to an end until its revival in 1939 as a suffragan see in the diocese of Oxford, itself founded only in 1542. Prior to this last date, the northern bank of the Thames, Oxfordshire and Buckinghamshire, remained in the diocese of Lincoln. The two sides of the Thames Valley were united when Berkshire was transferred to the diocese of Oxford in 1836 having been in the diocese of Salisbury, formerly Sherborne and Ramsbury, since 1078.

Up to the dissolution of the monasteries in the 16th century, the abbeys of Abingdon and Reading exerted great influence on their estates and churches. As these were widely scattered, many other abbeys, some French, held for a while a church or two along the Thames. Still other churches remained with the lords of manors, some royal. After the Dissolution, lords, old and new, came into possession, especially in Oxfordshire where the majority of manors were held by just four families, each of whom remained loyal to the Papacy: the Stonors, the Blounts of Mapledurham, the Powells of Sandford, and the Hides of Whitchurch, while the colleges of Oxford University were also endowed with many church estates.

The use of such possessions was much abused by absent rectors in the 18th century, as it had been at times in the medieval period. Following the ecclesiastical re-organisation last century, the majority of churches are now at the disposal of the bishop.

Today, Christian congregations are again small after the resurgence of beliefs in the 19th century, the schisms of earlier centuries and the mixture of faith and compulsion before. Yet nearly all the churches in the Thames Valley originated nine hundred years or more ago and whatever the vagaries and inconsistencies of passing generations, and the changes in liturgy, furnishing and decoration, so long as there are people acknowledging the Lord, their existence will be justified. They are places of living worship and as such subject to as much change in the future as in the past; their history did not close with the fossilizing restorations of the last century, nor will it now in order to satisfy secular antiquarian interests.

A few churches in the area are closed because of generally declining populations: Basildon, Mongewell and Newnham Murren. A few more may be closed in time, but others such as Burley, Benson and Radley are being challenged to take the Gospel to newcomers as Birinus did in the Thames Valley over thirteen hundred years ago.

CHAPTER II

Church Buildings

Following the general conversion of the Saxons to Christianity, churches were built for the larger settlements; smaller places continued to be served for some centuries by itinerant priests from minsters holding services in the open or in private dwellings.

In the Thames Valley region the churches would have been almost entirely of timber, wattle and daub, and thatch. This may even have been the case with the first abbey at Abingdon. Stone may have come into use following the first depredations of the Danes in the late 9th century, though some wooden chapels continued in use, until as late as 1200, in parts of Berkshire.

A further stimulus to more permanent buildings was the monastic revival of the late 10th century which was closely followed by renewed Danish raids in the early 11th century. So, before the Conquest, many churches were being built or re-built. Norman influence preceded William in many ways, including architecture; thus, down the Thames at Westminster, the great abbey church was completed for Edward the Confessor by 1065, very much in keeping with developments in Europe.

'Now (Edward the Confessor) laid the foundations of the church
With large square blocks of grey stone;
It foundations are deep,
The front towards the east he makes round;
The stones are very strong and hard;
In the centre rises a tower,
And two at the western front,
And fine and large bells he hangs there.
The pillars and entablature
Are rich without and within;

At the bases of the capitals
The work rises grand and royal,
Sculptured are the stones,
And storied the windows;
All are made with the skill
Of a good and loyal workmanship.
And when he finished the work
With lead the church he completely covers.
He makes there a cloister, a chapter-house in front,
Towards the east, vaulted and round,
Refectory and dormitory,
And the offices around.'

After the Conquest, Ermenfrid, a Norman bishop, imposed penances on all members of William's army according to the injuries or deaths caused. Lesser penances could be commuted by the giving of alms or, significantly, by contribution to church building. Other factors which induced the subsequent great building activity were the cultural pressures and desires of a 'superior' people establishing itself; the political involvement of Church and State; the concentration of power and material wealth in the hands of a few men; and the changes in the arts fostered by the monastic communities, the centres of learning at that time.

Returning to the Saxon parish, buildings were of the most basic kind, architecturally and decoratively; for the people a plain rectangular room sufficed in which to stand or kneel; for the altar and priest there was a smaller second room. In southern England, through the influence of the Continental missionaries, this chancel often had a rounded, or apsidal, eastern end. The two rooms were connected only by a small arched opening, both in the Saxon and early Norman periods. There is an example in the south aisle at Clewer; Purley still has its arch, though not in situ. At Cholsey there is a central Saxon tower with Norman arches, still relatively small; a similar arrangement, with arches smaller than at present, existed at Upton.

The reasons for small central towers and arches have yet to be fully established, but it may be that in the 10th and 11th centuries the typical cube altar — which in a large and important building would have stood under a ciborium — actually stood under the tower, an apse being used for the presiding priest's seat. It was the altar that provided the *raison d'etre* for a central tower, and when liturgical requirements changed and the altar was moved into an eastern chancel, so the

17

central tower's validity ceased, except where monastic arrangements and greater scale maintained its viability.

In a small church, such an altar arrangement under an arched tower would have facilitated veiling at two points in the Mass, a practice for which there is 10th and 11th century evidence.

From the early 12th century rectangular altars were being introduced, partly perhaps to provide more top surface for portable reliquaries and feretories, the 'relics' for which were becoming widely available, especially through pilgrimages to the Holy Land, Italy, Spain, France and Germany, and through the Crusades. In some instances this would have necessitated extending or rebuilding the apse or chancel to accommodate the larger altar.

Also, veiling was no longer required, when the Elevation of the Host was introduced in 1215 by the Lateran Council, which pronounced the dogma of transubstantiation. The resulting solemn celebration of the Mass with more elaborate ritual brought a further period of reconstruction, especially the enlargement of chancels in the early English style. Screens were installed to enforce the separation of people and altar, and proclamations such as that by Grosseteste, Bishop of Lincoln, 1235-54, forbade the laity to enter the chancel.

The adoption of these developments was never consistent from one church to the next, everything depending on the lay or monastic patron. It is very difficult therefore, in studying these buildings – as opposed to cathedral or monastic establishments – to argue either from the general to the particular or vice-versa, in matters of architectural and stylistic development. Each church needs to be examined and interpreted in the light of its own architectural and documentary evidence and in the light of these wider themes, due allowance being made for the many unknown factors which have contributed to its unique growth.

The churches with central towers covered in this survey may be divided into two groups: those with towers only, and those with transepts as well. To the former belong Upton and Iffley; to the latter, Cholsey, Dorchester and Hambleden (the towers of the last two have been removed). Cholsey appears to be Saxon whilst the others are of Norman foundation. For comparison, the churches with early west towers are as follows: Clewer, Bisham, Goring, Sutton Courtenay, Sandford, and St Michael's, Oxford. The latter is Saxon; the others are later Norman additions to early Norman or even Saxon buildings.

Western towers did in fact exist in their own right from the Saxon

18

period. It is possible that in a few cases early towers were incorporated in later buildings in new positions, (St. Mary's, Oxford; St. Helen's, Abingdon). Expediency rather than preference may also have fostered the west tower, for where a simple church already existed the introduction of a central one would have involved major rebuilding. Most of the churches in this area were just such simple buildings originally, with rectangular naves and chancels; the latter developed in the same manner as outlined for central-towered churches.

Transeptal plans were well developed in the larger buildings of the Saxon period, especially in Europe. Their translation to parish churches may have been compounded with the Saxon porticus. This was a small room erected off the nave, usually one to the north and one to the south. Initially they may have served as sacristy and vestry, then developing into chapels, partly through the private devotions of the priest, and partly through the limitation of one Mass to be said daily at the one altar. Where a church had more than one priest or a second Mass was required, additional altars became necessary. The existence of transeptal chapels is illustrated at St. Mary's, Cholsey and St. Mary's Hambleden. Some transepts, or side chapels, have since been absorbed into later aisles which again came into being because of the need for more altars, not it will be noted, to provide extra accommodation for the laity. Special altars were proliferated by chantry foundations and by numerous guilds and fraternities. Small churches housed new altars in the nave and wherever space could be found. This growth of aisles and chapels is well displayed at St. Helen's, Abingdon.

The overall development of most churches was completed in the 15th century, only for much of its justification to be swept away in the Reformation.

Since then most alterations have been of a cosmetic nature, except where larger churches were required to serve growing town populations of the 19th century, as at St. Giles', Reading. One other distinctive late development, particularly noticeable in this area, was the form of tower which appeared in the late medieval period: square, with polygonal buttresses, partly or wholly faced with flint and stone chequerwork.

Among the Thames Valley churches the earliest, and perhaps finest example is that at St. Laurence's, Reading, c. 1450. In the same genre are the towers at Henley, early 16th century; St. Mary's, Reading (1550-3); Dorchester (1605); St. Mary's, Wallingford (1653); Warborough (1666); and Remenham (1838).

A similar pattern arose with the increasing use of brick from the 16th century onwards; the church at Wargrave dates from 1635. Although

19

used in previous centuries for churches – generally as coursing material or rubble – brick only came into favour following the secular fashion set by such buildings as Wolsey's Hampton Court. Even then it tended to be confined to areas like the Home Counties and middle Thames region where there was local production from indigenous clays.

Dorney church tower is the earliest, dated to 1540; followed by Purley (1626); Staines (1631 and 1828); Pangbourne (1718); Hambleden (1721) refaced with stone and flint, (1883); Basildon (1734); and Tilehurst (1737). Most of these examples have stone dressings; flint was used in addition at North Stoke in 1726.

Brickwork may also be seen in the porches of Sutton Courtenay (early 16th century), and Dorney (1661).

Flint, being a widely available and durable material, is a very much in evidence. Its early use was as rubble; as a facing material it came into prominence in the 15th century and then again in the mid and late 19th century.

Good stone, except nearer Oxford, was always an expensive commodity, not only because of the skilled labour required but also because of the very high cost of transport. So the many lesser churches used local materials for rubble wall construction and local sources of chalk (clunch) for the small amount of dressed stonework. With increasing prosperity, more ambitious alterations were carried out, and better quality stone was brought from distant quarries, as far as possible by river.

Roofs are now generally tiled or, where low-pitched, covered with lead. There are no examples of thatch but many must have existed when straw was plentiful, if short-lived, and the skill was widely practised. Indeed, the majority of tiled roofs in the Thames region probably belong to the 19th century. Stone slating would have been a rarity in the area, except for churches of exceptional quality.

The latter epitomises the development of the Norman – more accurately, Anglo-Norman – architectural style with its rich stone decoration. Much other fine carving of the period, 1130-80, is in evidence at Horton, Cholsey, Crowmarsh Gifford, and St. Leonard's, Wallingford. In fact a large proportion of the churches in this survey have an item or fragment surviving from that period.

The style is also illustrated by the fonts at Upton, Clewer, Dorney, Hambleden, Purley, Mapledurham, Crowmarsh Gifford and Radley. Apart from a few early plain tub-fonts, the remainder tend to be typical panelled examples of the 15th, or 19th century Gothic types;

the exceptions are the lead fonts at Dorchester, Long Wittenham and Warborough.

Good stonework of later periods may be studied at Cholsey, Iffley and Greyfriars, Reading, where there is early English work. Decorated work may be seen at Dorchester and Sonning; and perpendicular work at St. Helen's, Abingdon and St. Mary's, Oxford.

Very little early woodwork has survived, just a fragmentary screen or two, a few bench ends, some plain roofs, consistent with the re-furnishings of the 17th century. There are however many good pulpits of that period, notably at North Stoke, Sutton Courtenay, St Helen's and St. Nicolas', Abingdon, and Marsh Baldon.

Most altars, and their appointments, being particularly susceptible to change, are of the late 19th or early 20th centuries as are the majority of other furnishings. Rarely do these merit special attention, excepting the work of Sir Ninian Comper which can be seen at Wooburn, Caversham and Iffley.

Examples of medieval painting are singularly lacking, though the few compensate through their quality. The major survivals, all of the 14th century are the Crucifixion at Dorchester, the many scenes at North Stoke and the Jesse roof panels at St. Helen's, Abingdon.

Stained glass, considering its fragility, is well represented, some at St. Michael's, Oxford, dates from 1290; other pieces of good quality can be seen at Shiplake (15th century); Dorchester (14th century); Radley (16th century); and Marsh Baldon (14th century).

Memorials, in many ways the most fascinating objects for study, include sculpture and decoration of exceptional quality and richness. In particular one recalls the superb 14th century knight-effigy at Dorchester, and the magnificent Hoby monuments of the late 16th century and early 17th century at Bisham. Many other fine examples, also of the 17th century to be seen at Egham, Dorney, Hurley, Hambleden, Henley, Reading (St. Laurence's), Tilehurst, Purley, Mapledurham, South Stoke and Radley, all testify to the newly-found wealth of the riverside estates and the advent of Renaissance man.

Brasses are very numerous, the majority being of poor 16th century craftsmanship; but there are several good earlier works including ones at Bray, Taplow, Harpsden, Sonning, Whitchurch, Dorchester and Little Wittenham.

The facets of a church building worthy of study are endless; the interested visitor will make many more comparisons than the few drawn briefly here and during the journey that now follows.

21

CHAPTER III

Staines to Windsor

If this were a real journey, the ideal vehicle would be undoubtedly the 'Thames' broad aged back'; the difference of scene and pace by boat has to be experienced to be understood. It is similarly pleasant on foot, though the loss of most ferries where towpaths cross the river makes for difficult travelling.

This journey, however, is primarily a figurative device since it seemed that the most appropriate way to 'look' at these churches was to leave them in their geographical context, especially as this would contribute significantly to an understanding of their origins.

So, beginning at Staines, the start of the Upper Thames from London, one travels from church to church, crossing the river from side to side as the situation dictates, until Oxford is reached.

The trafficked clamour and bustle amidst the jostle of old and new facades were always characteristic of Staines, a riverside market town on the great road from London to the South and West. It was an important route and river crossing long before the Romans built their road to Silchester; they used two bridges and an island to pass over the Thames, and maintained a post here aptly named Pontes. One of their milestones may have given rise to the name Staines, from the Saxon 'stana', stone. This is not to be confused with the London Stone, by the bridge, which was the first erected about 1285 to mark the limit of the City of London's authority over the river; here Upper and Lower Thames meet.

Just upstream from the bridge is a small backwater and a tributary stream near which stands the singular brick church of St. Mary, on a knoll. After the main street this area with its old buildings and trees is full of quiet charm.

As long ago as 675 A.D. – the year of Abingdon Abbey's founding – Erminildis, daughter of the King of Mercia, is recorded as having built a stone church here. Whatever rebuilding followed, the medieval

St. Mary's, Staines c. 1631

23

church has long since disappeared. In 1631 the plain west tower, of dark red brick, was built – one of several of that period to be found along the Thames Valley. Its parapet was reconstructed following bomb damage in World War II; the top storey belongs to 1828 when the rest of the church – the nave, aisles and chancel – was rebuilt in yellow brick, with a galleried interior, in a severe Gothic Revival manner. Churches of the same period are to be seen at Windsor and Egham.

The ancient highway that is now the A30 trunk road crosses the Thames and soon passes Ecga's homestead, the present town of Egham.

Amid the pleasant shopping centre, yet half-concealed behind great trees, is the church of St. John the Baptist. This distinctive building, with its late Georgian classical facades and west tower, was built by Henry Rhodes, 1817-20, to replace the old church which was in poor condition and could not accommodate the growing population.

Of that earlier church all that remains is the 15th century lychgate, formerly the porch, and a curiously lettered tablet in the south east chapel, apparently recording the rebuilding of the chancel in 1327 by John de Rutherwyke, Abbot of Chertsey. The abbey held the advowson in 1283 when it presented Walter de Isledon as vicar. A church would seem to have existed from at least the early Norman period.

A number of old monuments have been preserved including a brass of 1576; an Elizabethan crested wall plaque to Richard Kellifet; a singular portrait bust in an oval niche to the Lord Chief Justice, Robert Foster, who died in 1663; and most notably the two Denham memorials on the gallery stairways. One is a very unusual and impressive depiction in marble of a personal resurrection: Sir John Denham, Baron of the Exchequer d. 1638, is shown rising from the grave and casting off his winding sheet. The other in more conventional and charming form, shows Sir John's two wives, Cecile, d. 1612, and Eleanor.

The elegant galleried interior is a single volume with a simple shallow sanctuary at the east end. The fine canopied oak pulpit of the early 18th century was brought here from Suffolk in 1948. In the north aisle is a huge painted Royal Coat of Arms, dated the year of the monarchy's restoration, 1660.

From Egham, to the North, are the meadows of Runnymede and the island where Magna Carta was signed in 1215. That time was significant for Old Windsor, for in the siege of Windsor Castle, and the foraying around, the church was damaged, resulting in the building of the present tower and the chancel (of which only the east wall remains). These are the earliest remains, for in the middle of the 14th century the north and south walls of the nave and chancel were rebuilt, and it is from then that the distinguished flat-headed and traceried nave windows date. Subsequent alterations were few until the major restoration of 1863-4 by Sir Gilbert Scott who added the north chancel aisle and south porch, re-roofed the church and erected the handsome shingled broach spire, like that at Clewer. Gothic, Jacobean and Georgian furnishings were removed at that time, so that it is a rather plain interior today. Much 19th century wall painting has had to be obliterated, leaving only that at the west end.

There are no indications that the church was ever more than a simple nave and chancel in its earliest days; yet in Saxon and early Norman times Old Windsor was, in fact, Windsor, and apparently a town of some importance, with a Royal Palace. It is just possible that there was a second church, which might explain the unusual dual dedication to Ss. Paul and Andrew. But what is clear is that very shortly after the Conquest, Windsor Castle was established and becoming the royal residence inevitably attracted away trade; so Windsor became 'Old' in its decline and before 1200 the church was reduced, to being a chapel to St. John's 'new' Windsor. In these conditions of change it is not likely that a Norman church of distinction was built. Today it is quietly situated in its pleasant tree-screened churchyard, close to the river and away from the village centre.

Across the river and through the housing estates is the centre of Wraysbury village, sited on a stream on the low-lying river plain now pocked with gravel pits and reservoirs. This was Wigric's burgh long before the Conquest; in the 11th century the name is recorded as Wirecesberie.

Just off the main street, along a tree-lined track, is St. Andrew's church, very pleasantly situated with open fields to the south and the river. The church itself presents a rather hard and pretentious face, largely the work of Brandon in 1862. Then the west tower with its broach spire was rebuilt and the whole exterior refaced. Only inside is its age revealed: the arcade detailing suggests an early 13th century date, and the heavy piers themselves indicate earlier nave walls pierced through to join the newly built north and south aisles.

A church evidently existed at or immediately after the Conquest for Robert Gernon, the Norman lord of the manor, is recorded as having granted the advowson to Gloucester Abbey.

The only other early work surviving is in the font which seems to be a conglomerate of several periods.

In the 15th century the north chapel was added; this contains some late 17th century panelling, the same age as the oak pulpit.

Memorials of note include an unidentified brass to a knight (possibly John Brecknock, d. 1488), with an indent to his lady, under a double canopy; and a diminutive brass to John Stonor, d. 1512, generally described as an Eton College schoolboy but more probably a doctor of laws; and monuments to Harriet Paxton, d. 1794 and to William Gyll, d. 1806.

Similarly placed to Wraysbury is Horton – to the north east and almost a mile from the river – for its name probably describes a village or homestead on muddy land.

Near Horton Manor is St. Michael's church. The approach is from the north leading to a large porch with 15th century carved woodwork. Within, one is confronted by a splendid doorway of the mid 12th century which has wide mouldings with geometric enrichment. This opens directly into the nave which is pleasingly lit from the south aisle through the triple-arched arcade of about 1200. The western arch bears traces of red painting in the form of vine trails.

To the north of the nave is a chapel added in the early 15th century. The west tower was probably first built at that time, being partly reconstructed about 1580 when the brick and stone top storeys to the tower and stair turret were built and the bellchamber windows were inserted.

The chancel arch and possibly the rood-loft stair date from about 1500, but the chancel itself was rebuilt in 1875-6. At that major restoration the south aisle outer wall was also rebuilt, and a vestry was added.

At the west end is a simple tub font with only a rope-twist roll around the top edge for decoration; this belongs to the same period as the north doorway. Most of the other furnishings are of the late 19th or early 20th centuries.

It is likely that the lord of the manor in 1086, Walter de Windsor, erected a simple early Norman church which was remodelled in the mid 12th century, a common pattern of development.

The road to the river brings one to the attractive village of Datchet. From early times there was an important ferry here – often used as a short cut to Windsor and the Castle – which continued until the first bridge was erected in 1706. Closer to the long green is St. Mary's church which was almost entirely rebuilt by

Porch detail, St. Michael's, Horton.

27

North door, St. Michael's, Horton.

28

Brandon, 1857-60. The chancel was retained, and part of the plan probably reflects the earlier building. The church here in the 12th century was given to St. Alban's Abbey by the Pinkney family, lords of the manor from the Conquest.

Many memorials have survived including three tablets to members of the Wheeler family of 1626, 1633 and 1636.

From Datchet the Slough road passes over the M4 motorway into the now suburban area of Upton. Once there was a Saxon settlement here, and probably a church too. The present church of St. Laurence stands at a minor crossroads which were probably of greater importance before the growth of Slough. By 1100 or so the nave and central tower existed; the lower rubble-work coursing consists of the distinctive brown 'pudding stone' or conglomerate, and this use of such localised material is a feature of Saxon and early Norman building technique.

The tower is narrower than the nave and originally had smaller arches to east and west than those inserted in the 19th century; to the east there would probably have been a small apse but the altar may well have stood under the tower. The impressive vaulted chancel was built about 1160 and consists of two bays with diagonal ribs which bear contemporary painted decoration, albeit partially restored. Vaulting is rare in all parish churches, the only other examples in this group being at Iffley, the towers at Goring and Bray, and the porches of St. Michael's Oxford and St. Nicolas', Abingdon.

It would appear that the nave was lengthened westward about the same time as the chancel was erected. One factor most likely to have promoted this not inconsiderable redevelopment was the change of ownership to Merton Priory some time after 1125. Other features of the period are the pillar-piscina with its octagonal column marking the start of the transition to the Early English style, the font with its simple blank arcading around a tub-shaped bowl raised on a circular stem; and the north doorway.

In the following century a pair of carved oak arches were set up apparently across the tower's west archway, perhaps in conjunction with a rood; one of these arches is now preserved as part of the east wall of the south aisle.

Apart from the insertion of larger windows in the 15th century, little changed until the church fell into disrepair in the early 19th century, only being saved from demolition in 1835 by the conditional offer of £50 from a parishioner. By that time Slough was growing rapidly and

St. Laurence's, Upton, c. 1100

30

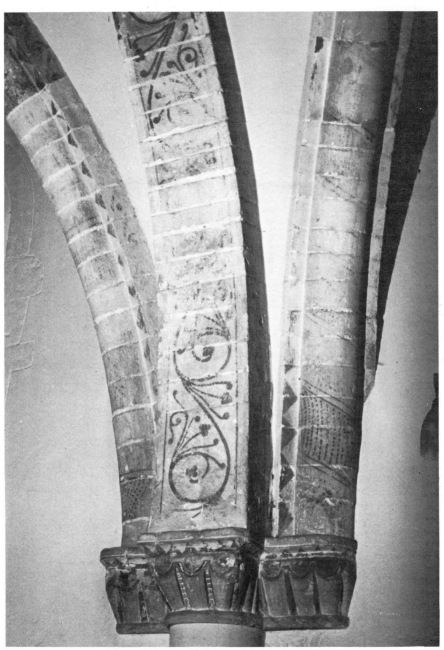

Vaulting, St. Laurence's, Upton.

Font, St Laurence's, Upton.

a new church, the predecessor of St. Mary's, was being built. Eventually in 1850-1, under the direction of Benjamin Ferrey, the church was restored with the addition of the south aisle. The south vestry and organ chamber date from 1879.

Under the tower, in a moderate niche, is a broken but nevertheless very fine alabaster carving of the Holy Trinity, dating from the 15th century. There is a brass of the same century, c. 1472 and two of the

Alabaster Trinity, St. Laurence's.

16th century, all to members of the Bulstrode family, in the south aisle.

Sir William Herschel, the astronomer who died in 1822, is commemorated by a mural tablet on the north wall of the tower.

Travelling on towards the river brings one to Eton and the privileged world of Eton College. In 1438 Henry VI purchased the advowson of the parish church of St. Mary's and in 1440 founded 'The King's College of our Lady of Eton beside Windsor'. The following year the magnificent college chapel was begun and towards the end of its building the old church, first mentioned in 1198, was demolished – perhaps to make way for the ante-chapel, 1479-82. The chapel served the parish until the present church of St. John the Evangelist was built in 1854.

It is remarkable that yet another magnificent chapel, St. George's Windsor, should exist so close; such is the result of the royal patronage based at the great castle and palace which so dominates the town and landscape today as it was intended to dominate the people in its much simpler beginnings.

William I built many castles to maintain his authority including those at Windsor, Oxford and Wallingford. Because of this, 'new' Windsor arose supplanting Old Windsor.

In the shadow of the castle, whose massive walls contrast so strongly with its delicacy, is the church of St. John the Baptist. This elegant 'Gothick' edifice replaced a medieval church in 1820-2, the architect being Charles Hollis. The interior is galleried on three sides, as at Egham, but was fundamentally altered by the addition of the polygonal apse in 1869-73.

The earlier church was of much the same size and plan but had a low central tower crowned by a 16th century wooden belfry and spirelet. The heavy stone arcades were apparently Norman; and as the first timber castle was only reconstructed in stone from 1165-79, it may be that this church belonged to the same period. Certainly it was well established by 1184, and in 1189-90 the advowson, formerly held with Old Windsor church, was granted to Waltham Abbey. An early reference of 1168 to the church and its maintenance of a leper hospital indicates that a building probably existed soon after the establishment of the castle.

As would be expected in an important town, indeed a royal borough, fraternities and guilds flourished in the medieval period so that there were several chantries and no less than ten side altars, in the parish church.

34

St. John the Baptist, Windsor.

35

Many monuments have survived from the 16th, 17th and 18th centuries. At the east end of the south aisle wall are two simple lettered stone memorials of 1509 and 1514. Nearby, Edward Jobson, d. 1605, is commemorated by a tablet with kneeling figures. Also to be noted are monuments to Richard Braham, d. 1618; Rebecca Southcot, d. 1642; and Hartgill Baron, d. 1673. In the main vestibule is a wall monument, with two busts in the pediment, to Mrs Nazareth Paget, d. 1666. Opposite is an early work by Scheemakers, the well known 18th century sculptor, to Topham Foot, d. 1712, but probably executed after 1730. A later work is that to Sir Thomas Reeve, d. 1735, with busts and putti, in the north vestibule.

The church possesses some splendid woodwork in the carved rails surrounding the Royal Pew; these were carved by Grinling Gibbons, c. 1680, for the castle chapel where they remained until 1788. Also in that chapel, until given to St. John's by George III, was the great painting of the Last Supper, attributed to Francis de Cleyn, 1588-1658, and now hanging in the west Gallery.

Unlike St. George's Chapel this church is not on the normal tourist route and is well worth a visit.

CHAPTER IV

Windsor to Maidenhead

Amid the growing environs of Windsor, on the other side of the M4
link, is the village church of Clewer, St. Andrew's, with a prominent
broach spire, similar to that of Old Windsor.

There is a hardness and crispness about the surfaces inside and out
which indicate heavy restoration, mostly the work of Woodyer from
1858 onwards. That is not to belie the surprise on entering the church
by the south porch to discover the large aisle with its late 12th century
arcade and font. Beyond is the nave and north aisle; to the east is a
south chapel with plain round arch, which with the south aisle, may
well have formed the original stone church of about 1100. At the same
time as the arcade was built the west tower was added.

The north aisle was not added until the 13th century, the new arcade
then being different from the south arcade; this may account for the
reconstruction of the north arcade, to match the earlier style, by
Woodyer during his restoration when he also reconstructed and extended the east end to provide a new chancel, organ chamber, vestry
and south porch. Just outside the porch is a very lively military
bas-relief on the end of a monument of 1819.

A chantry chapel dedicated to Our Lady is recorded about 1540.
This could have been a separate institution in the parish, or a building
attached to the church and since demolished or part of the church
itself, perhaps the south chapel. In the south wall of the chapel is a
14th century piscina and a tomb recess with ogee moulded arches. Such
a tomb could have provided the reason for a chantry here.

The chancel is rich with decorative Victorian furnishings in contrast
to the plain south aisle, with its modern crucifix over the east arch, and
the simple south chapel enriched only by the good early 20th century
reredos.

Upstream from Clewer on a large island site, is Windsor race-course.
On the north bank of the Thames is the tiny secluded hamlet of

37

St. Andrew's, Clewer, Tomb niche.

Boveney, 'the place above the island', where there are some well restored delightful old timbered houses. Close to the river bank, and reached only by footpath, is the simple, small church of St. Mary Magdalene set around with unattractive coppice.

This was once a chapelry in the parish of Burnham, being first mentioned in 1266. Its origins, so close to the river, may be connected with a wharf said to have existed here. The basic rubble structure would seem to belong to the 12th century. The west gable window, below the weatherboarded bell-turret, is the only original one, the rest having been inserted in the 13th and 15th centuries.

Inside it is just one room, the division between chancel and nave being provided by a low screen made up from 15th century and 17th century woodwork. Also of the 17th century is the wall panelling; the seating is earlier in date. The round stone font, with just an edge roll for detail, could be 12th century or 13th century.

A wall case contains many interesting fragments of 15th century alabaster carvings among which can be identified parts of scenes of the Assumption, Crucifixion and Resurrection; these may well have formed a reredos such as that at Drayton.

The altar setting is of the late 19th century, otherwise there is a good impression of an interior common to very simple churches before the restorations and enlargements of last century.

It is equally quiet and secluded around the ancient manor and the church of St. James' at Dorney which stand by a small stream about half-a-mile from the River Thames. There was a Saxon manor here which, by the time of the Domesday survey had passed into the ownership of Milo Crispin of Bec who also held Wallingford, North Stoke and Newnham Murren. About that time a manorial church was built which survives as the basic structure of the nave and chancel; the only identifiable detail is a blocked Norman window in the south chancel wall. The tower of red brick with stone dressings was built about 1540 but the base of pudding stone' and flint could indicate earlier origins. In 1661 the attractive brick south porch was added.

This whole building and its setting is so quietly captivating in its antiquity that it comes as no great surprise to find a charming interior displaying details and furnishings from all periods. Below the 17th century west gallery is the tub-shaped 12th century font with a low relief patterning of floreated crosses identical with that at Hambleden. An 18th century manorial pew, a fine hexagonal pulpit of the mid 17th century (from elsewhere), part of a 15th century screen, 16th and 17th century benches all exist happily side by side. 18th century small-paned windows light the nave by day; 19th century iron coronae still candle-light the nave by night.

In the chancel is 14th century work including a piscina, two low windows on either side of the chancel arch and the former chancel arch in the north wall around which are traces of an Annunciation painting discovered in 1932. This arch, with its 17th century doors, leads to a funeral chapel built for Sir William Garrard, who died in 1607. The great monument of decorated marble and alabaster depicts the kneeling Sir William facing his wife, Elizabeth. In the base are their seven sons and eight daughters; five children hold the conventional

Monument to Garrard family, Dorney.

Bray church, c. 1160.

41

skulls denoting death before their parents.

In the chancel, near the chapel, is an elaborately detailed wall monument to Jane, daughter of Sir James Palmer, who died in 1633.

The 19th century restoration was a conservative one, even retaining the plastered ceilings which give such a distinctive character to this church. And the careful embellishment with the recent addition of a modern embroidered frontal on the altar.

Not far from the peace of Dorney, the ribbon of the M4 provides a river crossing where none existed before, enabling one to quickly reach the delightful Thameside village of Bray. Of its early history very little is known. There was a Saxon manor which was held by the Crown, and evidently a church, recorded in the Domesday Survey. For a small farming settlement this was most probably a simple building comprising nave and chancel, the nave occupying much the same position as at present. There is a carved stone fragment of a horse on the wall of the former chantry chapel, now St. Michael's hall, in the churchyard. This may be comparable in date with the doorway carvings at Iffley and suggests this was part of a Norman rebuilding, c. 1160. This could have been prompted by the granting of the church to Cirencester Abbey in 1133. Further work seems to have taken place in the mid 13th century, judging by records of the old chancel arch removed in the 1859 restoration.

In 1293 Queen Margaret, wife of Edward I, was petitioned to enforce payment by the parishioners towards the church fabric. About this

Royal Arms of James I, Bray.

time a major reconstruction was begun involving the building of the south aisle and arcade and probably the north arcade and aisle also, although this was rebuilt in 1859. The west end was extended perhaps and also the present sanctuary with its piscina. The east end of the south aisle, the chapel of All Saints, was once separate, dating from the 13th century but rebuilt about 1500 together with the chancel, and the new chapel to St. Nicholas at the east end of the north aisle. The former chantry behind the church probably dates from this time also. The broad south tower was added about 1400 with its base forming a vaulted porch; it has been suggested that it was preceded by a Norman tower which would indicate that there was an early south aisle unless that were the nave itself as at Clewer (note that the aisles and nave are all equal in width), or that some earlier layout existed accounting for the somewhat unusual tower position.

The chapel and the chancel were extensively altered in 1859 by T. H. Wyatt, together with a heavy restoration of much else. In 1968 a new main altar was introduced into the nave because of the remoteness of the existing high altar, to the east of a long chancel. This striking, well detailed scheme was carried out by John Hayward.

The earliest memorials are two 13th century coffin slabs against the west wall; one has a cross on a stylised foliated stem with parts of a Norman-French inscription. There are many brasses, all worthy of study, including one on the north aisle north wall to Sir John de Foxley, d. 1378, and his two wives; at the foot is a fox couchant, a pun on Foxley. On the south wall of the south chapel is one to Sir William Laken, d. 1475, a justice of the King's Bench, with his wife.

Another William, William Goddard, is commemorated in a decorated alabaster wall monument in the sanctuary, showing him in effigy with his wife. He died in 1609 and by his will brought about the founding in 1623 of Jesus Hospital, Bray.

Of the same period is the carved and decorated Royal Arms of James I above the chapel screen in the south aisle. At the west end of that aisle stands the font, a typical example of the Perpendicular style. This has, however, been attributed to 1647 on the basis of the following churchwardens' account:

It.   payd to Mr. Winch of Fifield, for the new Phaunt .... 1.12.3.
It.   payd to Waul, the Joyner, for carrying home the Phaunt
      to his howse.. 0. 0.6.
It.   Payd more to Waule for the cover of the Phaunt, and

the piller, and for carving, painting, gyldeing,
setting up the same Phaunt .... 2. 2.0.

If this is the font it seems unlikely that a joiner would have set it up, being a mason's work. The reference to a pillar patently of wood, further suggests that this account is for a font, now disappeared, of a type quite common at that time, comprising a small marble bowl standing in or on a wooden column, and provided with a wooden cover. The existing font cover probably dates from the 16th century.

Only a mile away is the large town of Maidenhead. Once it was part of the ancient parishes of Bray and Cookham, and before 1297 was

Monument to William Goddard, Bray.

Brass of Sir John Foxley, Bray.

45

known as Soth Aylington. About 1270 a chapel was erected but not licensed because the two parishes concerned would not willingly relinquish their income from the village. A licence was granted in 1324 but the arguments and legal battles continued for centuries. Not until 1870 was it finally separated from Bray and Cookham.

With the building of a new wharf about 1296, the name was changed to Maydenhythe; and a bridge was built bringing the main road through from London with all its attendant trade and prosperity.

All the present churches are of the 19th century, built to meet the great expansion in that period, except for the church of St. Andrew and St. Mary Magdalene, a unique double dedication. This may have been the site of the original Maidenhead chapel; the present building of 1964-5 replaced one of 1822-5 which had to be demolished.

CHAPTER V

Maidenhead to Marlow

Upstream from Maidenhead Bridge is Boulter's Lock; on the Buckinghamshire side the bank becomes steeply wooded to flank the whole of the beautiful Cliveden reach. On top of the southern end of this scarp is the imposing Tudor style mansion of Taplow Court and in front of the house are the remains of an old churchyard, and a 7th century Saxon burial mound, a surprising survival on such a developed site. This is thought to be Taeppa's hlaw or barrow. The 11th century place-name is Thapelau.

Excavations have revealed occupation of this site from pre-Roman times. The Saxon manor was held by Asgot, from Earl Harold, before the Conquest, and it would seem likely that a manorial church could have existed then. In 1197 the manor and church were granted to Merton Priory who held them until the dissolution.

The church was demolished in 1828 and a new brick one to St. Nicholas built in the village; this in turn was rebuilt in stone in 1912 to the design of Fellowes-Prynne. The interior has a very impressive stone chancel screen in the Gothic manner.

Surviving from the original church are 17th century panelling in the north transept, the font, and a number of brasses. The font is of the table-top type, characteristic of the late 12th century. The shallow square bowl has blank arcading around it (the original bowl stands nearby) and is supported on a circular column on a square base with corner leaf-details; originally there would have been four corner columns.

In the south chapel floor are set the brasses which include the earliest surviving civilian brass in England, c. 1350, to Nichole de Aumberdene, which takes the form of a floreated cross with his effigy in the head. There are also three good figures to Richard Manfeld, d. 1455, his brother and sister.

The next crossing of the river from the Chiltern hinterland, down the

Bourne valley to Berkshire and the South must have been one of the principal reasons for the settlement established in the 4th and 5th centuries by the Saxons on earlier Bronze Age and Roman sites, and known by the 8th century as Cotham or Coccham, now Cookham, and remembered in Cockmarsh to the north. Christian missionaries would have been at work here from the mid 7th century and by 700 A.D. there was a monastery, among other estates, owned by the kings of Mercia; King Aethalbald gave it to the canons of Canterbury in 735 A.D.

With the presence of a religious community the existence of a parish church on the present site seems certain. It has been suggested that parts of the chancel east wall belong to an 8th century church but the evidence is scanty. Cookham with its royal estates was of some importance for the King's Great Council or Witenagemot was held here in 997 A.D. The Norman Kings took over these estates. Holy Trinity Church lies only a few yards from the main road leading to the bridge. Its nave and chancel were rebuilt by 1140, a rather late date which suggests that there was a good building here at or soon after the Conquest. A window in the north wall of the nave survives from this period. In the north wall of the sanctuary is a squint, which related to the cell of an anchoress who lived here from 1171-1181, giving her life to the worship of God. Presumably on her death the north Chapel was

Holy Trinity, Cookham.

Lady Chapel, Holy Trinity, Cookham.

49

built on the site hallowed by her service. This was extended to the west, forming St. Catherine's Chapel about 1220. A blocked north doorway has, outside, its original fine mouldings. Some fifty years later, the south arcade and the south aisle were begun, and extended to the east to form St. Clement's chapel. The work took some thirty years and the detailing reflects the changes in style during that time. Sir George Young wrote: 'In its proportions I think it nothing less than perfect. How well our Cookham builders judged their exquisite material. How grandly they arranged their lights and shades'.

The roof too is of that date, having been concealed until 1960-4. The chapel, stripped at the Reformation, stood disused till its restoration in 1945.

Likewise the north Lady Chapel was restored to use in 1970 having been the organ chamber and vestries for over a hundred years.

About 1400 the chancel was largely rebuilt, and early in the 16th century the substantial west tower with its prominent stair turret was added. The lower walls outside are faced in an original chequerwork of stone and flint.

In the 17th and 18th century there were several repairs mostly in brick, and in the 1860's and subsequently, major restorations were carried out.

There are several brasses, from the late 15th century onwards; they are mostly robustly executed, particularly those of 1520 to Robert Pecke and his wife, to be seen on the tomb chest against the chancel north wall. It is surmounted by an elaborate canopy, not unlike one at Bisham, which does not seem to have been made specifically for this tomb chest. There are other good monuments of the 16th, 17th 18th and 19th centuries and good work in the traditional vein of this century, especially the lectern. In the nave Sir Stanley Spencer's 'The Last Supper', painted in 1920, is worthy of special attention.

Below Cookham bridge, on the weir stream, is Hedsor wharf, near where remains of Romano-British pile dwellings were found in 1894. Behind is the north end of the wooded scarp which began at Taplow to the south. Similarly situated to Taplow Court and the old church is Hedsor Priory and the small church of St. Nicholas, which is most beautifully sited with a fine view over the Thames Valley. The 19th century house is the site of earlier manor houses dating back to the Saxon period. 'Heddes bank' provided a possessive origin for Hedsor.

The early history of the church is obscure but a building probably existed soon after the Conquest and the present nave and chancel may well reflect the original plan. It was and has remained a very simple building serving a small parish and a minor manor. About 1600 the church was 're-edified' by Roland Hynd, and then in 1862 a substantial restoration added a north aisle and apparently a south baptistery – unless it was a former porch. The Gothic style furnishings of the late 19th century are very complete, and included chancel wall decoration until it proved necessary to obliterate it in recent years.

Nearby the chalk hills are cut by the river Wye running down from High Wycombe to join the Thames at Bourne End. On the Wye stands Wooburn, literally the 'winding stream', with St. Paul's church battling ponderously against the 'dark satanic mills' of the last century. Behind the church are some pleasant cottages and houses – the old village nucleus.

The Saxon manor passed to Remigius, Bishop of Dorchester and then of Lincoln; subsequent Bishops of Lincoln maintained a palace hereabouts and held the advowson of the church until 1547.

Outwardly St. Paul's is very much the work of Butterfield in his restorations of 1856-7 and 1868-9. It has a spacious interior with massive arcades dating originally from the late 12th century when the church comprised nave, aisles and chancel. The massiveness is well complemented by a large and ornate rood screen of 1899 by Sir Ninian Comper.

Apparently in the 14th century the north chapel was added and the chancel rebuilt and about 1442 the west tower was erected.

There are five brasses, including one of a priest in cope and amice, Thomas Swayn, a prebendary of Aylesbury and chaplain to the Bishop of Lincoln, who died in 1519.

Westward from Bourne End is Well End, near where Little Marlow nunnery stood from the 13th century. The secluded village of that name is a mile further west on a stream, and away from the low-lying river meadows. Its origins lie with Marlow to which the land belonged till after the Conquest, but it may be assumed that there was a Saxon settlement here which duly became a separate Norman manor held from the Earl of Gloucester.

The church of St. John the Baptist presents an attractive if mouldering appearance. Entry is by a 16th century timber north porch into the north aisle; this was added in the 14th century to the original 12th century church of which the earliest remnant is the round-headed plain arch between the chancel and south chapel. If this arch is in its original position then the early plan is somewhat obscure. Only a little later is

51

Exterior, Little Marlow Church.

the simple pointed chancel arch and possibly the font too.

About 1275 the north wall of the chancel was rebuilt with very fine windows having moulded and shafted splays. Of a similar date is the trefoil-headed recess by the pulpit with dog tooth decoration; its original purpose is not apparent. When the north aisle was added the west tower was also built, possibly replacing an earlier one. In the 15th century the south aisle was added and joined to the south chapel in which a new east window was inserted. Other windows of this period are in both aisles. Plaster ceilings were removed from both chancel and chapel in 1902 to reveal 15th century timbering.

The arch to the tower belongs to its 14th century rebuilding; outside, new belfry windows were inserted in the 16th century.

Much was restored in 1866, but 17th century and 18th century furnishings were removed. Further work was undertaken in 1902 including the replacement of the dormer windows in the nave roof.

In the very pleasing south chapel is an arched tomb recess through to the chancel. The slab bears a brass to Nicholas Ledewich, d. 1430, and his wife Alice with an inscription and shields; his figure is now missing. In the chapel window are to be seen several good fragments of

15th century stained glass.

Between Little Marlow and its namesake now runs an elevated bypass affording fine views of the river scenery, and providing welcome relief to the lovely town and its famous suspension bridge. The latter was built between 1831 and 1836 following a succession of timber bridges, the earliest recorded in 1227. It is notable that All Saints' Church is very close by, this 19th century building occupying the site of a church of 12th century foundation or earlier. Such siting by an important crossing is common and this, with the alignment of the town which had been established for many centuries seems to belie the suggestion in the Victoria Counties Histories that the bridge was once further down river, unless this was in the Saxon period when the existence of a bridge would be exceptional, though not impossible. Marlow itself existed then, and is recorded as early as 722 A.D. as Merelafan. The meaning, 'lake remains', is obscure but could refer to reclaimed marshy land or to a former pile settlement. Neolithic, Bronze Age, and Romano-British remains have been dredged from the river, indicating very early settlement here.

It became a market town of some importance, and a borough in 1299 electing two members of Parliament. The old church is recorded as having comprised chancel, nave, north aisle, south aisle with a projecting chantry of the Guild of the Blessed Virgin Mary, and a west tower, the latter being Norman, similar to that at Bisham. It had a wooden spire in the 16th century, which was replaced in 1627, and finally collapsed with part of the tower late in 1831. As the church had been increasingly subject to flooding, and had been ill-repaired in the 18th century, it was demolished and a new building of brick and stone erected to the design of of C. F. Inwood, 1832-1835.

G. E. Street added the chancel in 1875-6 and the arcades in 1881-2; and J. Oldrid Scott supplied the finishing touch in his spire of 1898-9. It is the spire which compensates for a somewhat bleak interior relieved only by numerous memorials. Some come from the old church, the earliest being a typical small example with kneeling figures, to Katherine Willoughby, d. 1597. In the tower narthex is one to Sir Miles Hobart who died as a result of a coach accident in 1632, having been a Member of Parliament, the Commons voted £500 for the monument in 1640.

Three fine brasses were lost, but rubbings exist in the collections of the British Museum and the Society of Antiquaries.

The advowson was granted by the lord of the manor, one Robert

53

All Saints, Marlow, Bucks.

Fitz Hamon, before 1107 to Tewkesbury Abbey who held it until 1247, apart from a brief seizure by King John in 1203; it then rested with the Earls of Gloucester as lords of the manor until 1494 when it was returned to the Abbey. In 1541 it was granted to Gloucester Cathedral, and in 1855 transferred to the Bishop of Oxford.

CHAPTER VI

Marlow to Henley

Just half-a-mile away over the bridge is Bisham village; the church of All Saints' stands right on the river bank and is a familiar sight to river-farers. Bistesham or Bustlesham are the earliest recorded names, Saxon in origin, of the 10th or 11th century. The early manor was presumably at Bisham Abbey which was a preceptory of the Knights Templars in the 12th century; an Augustinian Priory from 1337, and a Benedictine Abbey only from 1537-40 when it passed to the Hoby family whose splendid memorials are such a prominent feature of the church. It may be observed that the church stands away from both the Abbey and the present village, and it would be interesting to discover the reason for its site, especially so close to the river.

The earliest part of the church is the square tower dated to about 1160 by the main features of the belfry windows and the tower arch. The windows were restored in 1962 with some of their original bold nail-head ornament; the tower arch has several types of decoration worth comparing with those at Clewer.

Before 1856 there was a large west door and porch of unknown date. The tower exterior is a marvellous patchwork of clunch stone and rubble; flint and brickwork. Up to 1905 this was all covered with plaster, as of course were most of our smaller churches until the 19th century. The brickwork parapet and quoining were probably carried out in the 16th century. The need to replace the quoins suggests a failure of the rubblework corner construction, a point more applicable to Saxon work – unless weathering of the soft chalk was the reason.

Of the rest of the church there are no remains or records, except that prior to the 1849 restoration the nave was its present length and the chancel was some ten feet shorter. The Hoby chapel to the south east had been added in the late 16th century, and a short south aisle in the early 19th century. In 1849-50 the nave and chancel were rebuilt and in 1856 the south aisle was rebuilt and opened into the Hoby chapel

The Hoby Tomb, Bisham.

57

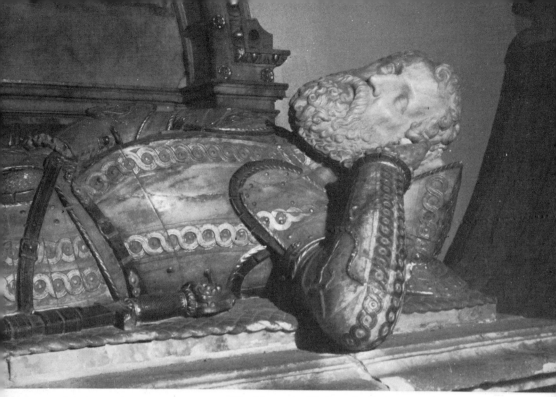

Sir Thomas Hoby, d. 1566.

with its glowing heraldic glass of 1609, and richly important monuments. The largest, against the south wall, is to Lady Elizabeth Russell, d. 1609, and depicts the familiar full-dress style complete with pillared canopy and kneeling figures of herself and her children. More restrained is the memorial she erected to her first husband, Sir Thomas Hoby, d. 1566, and his half-brother, Sir Philip, d. 1558, who lie side by side in languorous fashion, superbly detailed in their marble captivity, on a tomb chest and framed by a semi-circular canopy.

One of the most singular monuments is a sublime obelisk with swans supernal, surmounted by a heart, all on an armorial base. This is to the memory of Margaret, wife of Sir Edward Hoby, who died in 1605.

In the north aisle chapel is a monument very like one at Cookham; it dates from the early 16th century but came from Penmynnydd church, Anglesey, and was placed here when the chapel was built. The well carved canopy has a delicately traceried vault.

Close by it is an early 16th century reredos, with poorly painted saints, perhaps of East Anglian origin, and also given to the church.

An elaborate marble memorial to a kneeling Eton boy, George

Margaret Hoby monument d. 1605.

Kenneth Vansittart, who died in 1904 aged 14, echoes in Gothic style the monument to Lady Elizabeth.

On the Berkshire side amidst river meadows lies Hurley, a small secluded village which reveals some of its origins in the remains of a priory. In 1086, Bishop Osmund dedicated the village church of St. Mary for the use of a priory, a cell of the Benedictine Abbey of Westminster. He did this at the instruction of Geoffrey de Mandeville who, as a supporter of William I, had received many estates including Hurley, known as Herlie. Before this it would seem that a church or chapel already existed, possibly from as early as the late 7th century, for there was an important ford at this place. It is evident that a stone church existed before the Conquest – parts possibly remaining in the

Reredos 16th century, Bisham.

present south wall – which may have been ransacked during the Danish incursions up the Thames, which began in 870, the first attack on Wessex; again in 894, and perhaps in 1013 on their way from London via Wallingford, to Bath.

The present church of St. Mary the Virgin was formed from the nave of that priory church after the dissolution. The Norman or Saxon plan was probably that of a large cruciform building, which was extended and altered in the 12th, 13th and 14th centuries. Pevsner has commented on the Saxon proportions of the nave; this may be no more than evidence of the overlapping of the Saxon/Norman cultures and the continuation of the former under Norman rule; otherwise it might indicate an unusually large Saxon church, which could also have been of monastic foundation though there is no documentary evidence for this at present. The distinctive features remaining are late Norman, 1160-1200: the south and west doorways, much restored in 1852; and the west window fully restored in 1963. There was a major restoration in 1852, when the stone east screen was built with a vestry behind.

The font, which from its detailing was carved in the late 14th or

St. Mary's, Hurley, Berks.

61

early 15th century, is octagonal with traceried panels; it is unusual in its overall shape which is that of a tub-font. This peculiar combination suggests the possibility of this being an earlier font recut, for which there are precedents.

A major feature is the striking Lovelace monument in the sanctuary, restored between 1964-66. It is in fact two monuments, for the figures are of Richard Lovelace, d. 1602, and his son Sir Richard, (both surviving from a destroyed monument), whilst the background is to John Lovelace, d. 1588, and his wife, d. 1579, whose plaque is now well below the floor level which was raised in the 19th century restoration.

Today the church is well-ordered and well cared for, befitting its prominent place in people's lives throughout the centuries.

From Hurley, across the river, there was a ford, preserved in the name Harleyford on the north bank, which would seem to have formed part of an important west trade route from prehistoric times.

The Danes, in their incursions of 870-871 A.D. and 894-895 A.D., may well have used it, and indeed, its importance may have led to the establishment of a Danish camp on the north side, remembered in Danesfield, the site of earlier camps. The importance of a ford as a communication link undoubtedly fostered settlement nearby, such as Medmenham. Other factors such as south-facing slopes, the presence of water and readily mined flints, must have made this an attractive site from very early times, and there have been archaelogical discoveries to support this.

It is very probable that a church was established on a pagan religious site, about 640 A.D. by Bishop Birinus or one of his brethren. Because of its position it is likely that it was pillaged by the Danes in the late 9th century, and possibly again in the early 10th century. After the Norman Conquest the manor came into the hands of the Bolebec family. A descendant, Hugh de Bolebec II, rebuilt the church about 1150, probably a simple one consisting of a nave and chancel. All that is identifiable is the south doorway and blocked north doorway. He also founded the nearby Abbey of St. Mary's close to the river, and in due course the abbey held the patronage for three centuries. It was through one of the abbots that Sir Reginald Bray K.G., builder of Henry VII's chapel at Westminster, and St. George's chapel, Windsor, in the late 15th century came to alter much of the church, adding a new chancel, continuous with the nave, and a west tower, and renewing the nave roof. Prior to this a chantry chapel had been built in 1425; it fell into disuse and was eventually demolished in the 18th

Lovelace Monument, Hurley.

63

century.

A major restoration took place in 1839; internal alterations were made in 1906, 1925 (when the transept was built), 1937 and 1958. The open interior created by Sir Reginald Bray stems from the late medieval preference for a single-volume building, without an architectural division between chancel and nave. Because of this the tie-beam overhead was used to support a rood, as evidenced by dowel marks.

Other woodwork of note is the pulpit, the panels of which are elaborately carved with representations of the Nativity and Annunciation; these date from the early 17th century and either came from elsewhere, or belonged to a pulpit which was removed at the 1839 restoration.

There are brass memorials of the early 15th century, and wall-monuments and plaques of the 19th and 20th centuries. There is also a small hatchment of Anne Borlase, who died in 1677; this is a rare early example, the majority surviving being of the 18th and 19th centuries. In a window on the north side of the nave are four 16th century stained glass medallions of European origin brought here in 1839.

Further west, and a short way up a lovely small valley lies Hambleden, a compact village of cottages, church, manor and inn nestled around a small 'square' or 'green'. Here the scenery is more Chiltern than Thames Valley as the low wooded ridges drop to the river.

There is no direct evidence of pre-Conquest settlement though the valley was occupied at other points from the earliest times, and its sheltered position, stream, and proximity to the river and a trade route must have made it a favourable site.

The Norman lord began a substantial church, which by the mid 12th century had a nave and chancel with a central tower, and possibly transepts, as at Cholsey. The north transept was enlarged (or built) in the early 13th century, and much alteration took place in the early 14th century, when the chancel was lengthened, new windows inserted, and the piscina and sedilia carved. The nave and south transept were also altered.

In 1703 the central tower either collapsed or was demolished. As a result, between 1719 and 1721 a new west tower of red brick and flint was built to a design presumably drawing inspiration from the towers of Reading, Henley and High Wycombe. In 1883 it was fully encased in stone and flint, and heightened. Work of restoration, addition and

Hambleden Church.

Alabaster panel c. 1450, Hambleden.

alteration took place in 1859, 1883, 1906 and 1915, and interior decoration in the 1950's all resulting in the fine church of St. Mary the Virgin.

Close to the main entrance stands the great stone font, a virile example of Norman work, c. 1120-50, being a cylindrical tub with a strong bas relief patterning of floreated crosses. Here St. Thomas de Cantilupe, the last Englishman to be canonized before the Reformation, was baptized.

There are several small brasses of the 15th, 16th and 17th centuries.

In the tower is a wall monument to Ralph Scrope, d. 1572, and in an earlier Easter Sepulchre recess in the chancel, a table tomb to Henry, son of Lord Sandys, d. 1555. Particularly noteworthy is the Cope D'Oyley monument in the north transept aisle, this is in alabaster and shows Sir Cope D'Oyley, d. 1633, with his wife, d. 1618, both kneeling with their ten children. Other treasures are a 15th century carved and decorated alabaster panel of the Nottingham school, representing the Adoration of the Christ Child, and a painting, the Virgen de la Faja, by Murillo, on loan from Viscount Hambleden.

Returning down the little valley to the picturesque weather-boarded mill at Mill End, where a ferry used to cross to Aston

Sir Cope D'Oyley d. 1633.

and so reach Remenham, the nearest crossing now is at Henley, except for the footpath over the lock. Thus Remenham today is small and remote, standing at the foot of Remenham Hill as it slopes down to the river. But records indicate the existence of a bridge from the 13th century, and a chapel of Hurley Priory here at that time. The nature and direction of the route provided by this bridge is open to conjecture. In combination with the Aston ferry, it may have been a means of cutting off the loop in the river, or possibly it was part of a route from Hurley via older tracks to Aston and Remenham, crossing towards Lower Assendon and Bix (ways now non-existent) and on to Wallingford and the west.

The church of St. Nicholas, Remenham, would appear to date from shortly after the founding of Hurley Priory in 1086, for excavations last century revealed foundations of an apsidal east end and these are still partly to be seen at the base of the present apse. The apse is peculiar to the early period and soon ceased to be used. As the manor would have passed to a Norman after the Conquest, the foundation of a church shortly after is to be expected. The probable existence of an earlier Saxon manor, especially with the river crossing, raises the possibility of there having been a Saxon church.

Today's church however dates largely from 1870 when there was a major restoration, and the south aisle was added. In 1892 vestries were added, and soon after an organ installed in the former Noble family pew. A tower was probably an addition to the early simple nave-and-apse chapel in the late 15th century but whether the present tower outwardly represents it or is largely of 1838 origin (according to Pevsner) is difficult to decide. Either way, it has a strong affinity in its buttresses with those of the Henley and Reading churches.

The few other features include two late brasses, and an intricate wrought iron screen made in Italy in 1873.

By following the river south one reaches Henley bridge and there, immediately on the other side, stands the church of St. Mary the Virgin raised on an embankment and rising above the clustered roofs of this attractive market town.

The distinguished stone bridge, built in 1786, and its predecessors, was the site of an early ford and an important medieval route from London via Maidenhead to Wallingford, Dorchester, Abingdon and the west.

Henley, the high glade, suggests Saxon settlement on the wooded hills behind the town hall. This would have been a tribe of West Saxons whose chief town was Bensington (Benson); it is not surprising

68

St. Nicolas, Remenham.

therefore, to find the hamlet of Henley in the possession of the manor of Bensington in the 11th and 12th centuries.

Possibly monks from Dorchester founded, at or near the present church, a simple chapel to serve travellers making the river crossing; this could have happened when Dorchester was still a cathedral or after 1070 when it became an abbey.

In 1204 King John appointed Aumericus de Harcourt as rector, the first recorded appointeent.

Henry III gave the patronage to his brother, Richard of Cornwall, in 1244. Thirty years later it passed to the Bishop of Rochester, with whom it remained until 1852. It was then granted to the Bishop of Oxford.

Of this early church there are no remains or records until 1272 when contributors towards its building or repairing were granted release from year-long penances. It seems that the church then comprised a nave, where stands the present one, with narrow aisles and a chancel. The north and south nave arcades are for the most part the same time, early English. The aisle width is probably indicated by the surviving west end of the south aisle. It is unusual in a large church with aisles, to find no apparent indication of a tower. It is not inconceivable that there was a small central one, its eastern wall represented by the wall above the chancel arch, and accounting perhaps for the easterly pair of Perpendicular style columns which would have replaced heavy piers when such a tower was removed.

Between 1398 and 1420 there was much alteration including the rebuilding of the north aisle to a greater width, with the eastern chapel dedicated to Our Lady the Blessed Virgin Mary. Then a late Decorated arcade was made between this and the chancel. The Lady chapel was restored, following the moving of the organ, in 1964.

About 1460, on the north side of this rebuilt aisle the lovely chantry chapel, dedicated to St. Leonard, was erected by John Elmes of Bolney Court. This is a fine quality Perpendicular building in dressed stone.

In 1910 it was restored to use, having been a vestry during the 19th century, and was refurnished again in 1970. The good wrought iron screen is also of recent date. Towards the end of the 15th century the south or Jesus chapel was built in the Perpendicular style, and opened into the chancel. The first record of the Jesus altar is in 1498; other medieval altars existed, dedicated to St. Katherine, St. Clement, St. Nicholas, and St. Ann.

In the early 16th century the splendid tower was built at the west end of the north aisle. Outside it has high octagonal turrets, 118 feet

Nave, St. Mary's, Henley.

Monument, Lady Perriam d. 1621.

to the top. The south-east turret had to be rebuilt in 1868 after being struck by lightning. This flint and stone tower is very similar to those at St. Mary's and St. Laurence's, Reading and should also be compared with those at Hambleden, Remenham and Wallingford (St. Mary's). Henley's tower has been attributed to the benefaction of John Longland, born here and sometime Bishop of Lincoln. At about the same time as the tower, presumably, the chancel arch was reconstructed with the eastern nave arcade piers referred to earlier. This work culminated evidently in the provision of a new rood in 1519.

In the early 17th century, a new font was installed; this remarkable and rare piece now stands near the back of the church, having been displaced by a 19th century font installed in an imposing baptistery under the tower. The interior was filled with box pews in the 18th century, and the odd extension to the south aisle was made. Galleries were added in the early 19th century. These were all replaced in the major restoration which took place between 1852 and 1856. An outer north aisle was added, the floor renewed, the clerestory built (except for the east end which existed and determined the new roof construction), the chancel re-roofed, the west window inserted, the baptistery made below the tower; and the whole church re-furnished.

The chancel was elaborately re-decorated in 1890 and new choir stalls provided. The following year the great painting of the Adoration of the Lamb over the chancel arch was carried out by Rev. E. Geldart. In 1898 the marble pulpit was installed. As a memorial to the dead of the First World War, the intricately carved rood screen was erected in 1920.

The major monument stands by the entrance to St. Leonard's chapel and is a very large marble architectural piece framing the reclining alabaster effigy of Lady Elizabeth Perriam who died in 1621. She founded a school in Henley which met for a time in the ancient chantry house outside the east end of the church.

73

CHAPTER VII

Henley to Reading

Just a mile south, on the fringes of Henley, lies Harpsden, as small today as it must have been in its infancy. This is a manorial settlement, Harpsden Court with the farm and church making one group; and houses and school making a second group half-a-mile away. Harpendene or Harpeden denotes the valley of the Harp, a small stream fed by an underground stream discovered recently close to the west end of the church.

It is not known if a Saxon church existed, but probably by 1100 there was a simple stone building comprising nave and chancel (or apse). Of that period the blocked plain south doorway remains, and the piscina in the chancel. The font dates from the first half of the 12th century; the 'rope' band is decorated in the same manner as on the Mapledurham font and the Sonning pillar piscina.

Probably in the mid 14th century some new windows were inserted. An interesting example, with a detached inner column is now in the north aisle; until 1848 this was in the north wall and was moved when the aisle was built, necessitating the cutting down of its arches to fit under the low roof line. This window contains a few pieces of old glass. Also in the 14th century the chancel was rebuilt and lengthened eastward, and the nave re-roofed.

Apart from the erection of the aisle in the 1848 restoration, the nave was extended westward and the north tower was added so transforming this church. Today it presents a typical flint and stone exterior with a very pleasant whitened and well-ordered interior. The dedication is to St. Margaret of Antioch, but may have been to St. Peter before the 14th century.

There are several brasses, two worthy of special note: one to an unknown knight and his lady dated to between 1425 and 1460 and not in their original matrix; the armour is very like that of the Fyton brass, 1434, at Sonning. The other to a rector, Walter Elmes, dressed in a eucharistic vestment, who died in 1511. Under a pointed arched recess in the south chancel wall is an early 14th century stone effigy to a knight, similar in style to that of the 'Holcomb' effigy in Dorchester Abbey. Three quarters of a mile to the east stands Bolney Court and there by the river, at a wharf called Bulhythe, stood a church until the 15th century; in 1453 that parish was united with Harpsden.

Further up the winding river, and on a steep wooded bank as at Caversham, is the church of Ss. Peter and Paul, Shiplake. As at Harpsden and so many other places, a church was provided by the manor at Shiplake Court close by. The name apparently refers to a place for washing sheep – presumably down the slope at the river where a small stream joins it.

It is very likely that a homestead existed from Saxon times, if not earlier. A church is first recorded when in 1163 Walter Gifford, Earl of Buckingham gave it to Missenden Abbey. Of that building there are no discernible parts for the extensive restorations and additions of 1822 and 1870 completely changed its character. The latter works were under the direction of G. E. Street, and included the erection of the north aisle with its west tower, and the provision of the Norman style font. In the earlier restoration, some wall-paintings were discovered but not preserved.

It is suggested that the south aisle, clearly the oldest part of the building was the original church (see Clewer) but one would expect a nave and small chancel; alterations, including demolition, could however, account for there only being the aisle nave. The foundation of the present nave is attributed to Richard, Earl of Cornwall, brother of Henry III, suggesting a date between 1242 and 1275. In the south aisle is a piscina which could belong to that period, and could have served the altar of St. Nicholas which existed in the church in the medieval period.

There are several interesting furnishings presented to the church in the 19th and 20th centuries including a 15th century Italian processional cross, and 15th century French canopied chair. The greatest acquisition was the late 15th century stained glass which was rescued from St. Bertin's church at St. Omer in northern France and given to the vicar of Shiplake in 1828. This, in all its beautiful colour and drawing, was pieced together as far as possible and is to be seen in the east and south-east windows of the chancel, and the east, south-east and west windows of the south aisle. The best is in the triple lancets over the high altar. Left: from top to bottom, Coronation of the Virgin

75

Mary; St. Barbara; St. Anthony. Centre: St. Peter; St. Andrew; an abbot (St. Omer?); an apostle or saint; a monk perhaps St. Benedict. Right: Charlemagne; St. Catherine; St. John the Evangelist. There is one late brass of the 16th century, also a late 16th century wall monument with half-effigy of Andrew Blunden, lawyer.

About one mile away to the east, on the other side of the river, stands Wargrave church. There is a ferry for there are no bridges between Henley and Sonning.

The existence of a church at Weregrava before 1066 would seem probable, even a building of stone.

Prior to 1085 the manor, a royal demesne, was in the possession of Edith, wife of the late King Edward, known as the Confessor. Records show that the patronage held with the manor, was granted by the Crown to the Abbey of Mont St. Michael in Normandy, probably by 1085, and lasting till about 1125 when it was transferred to the new abbey at Reading. With this change of ownership there was a rebuilding resulting in a church with a nave and chancel, possibly with transepts. The only remains of this are the north doorway, which has some carving, and traces of arcading in the north wall which had been concealed since 1849 when there was a major restoration involving the removal of the south transept and the building of a south arcade and aisle.

In the intervening centuries there were only minor alterations. The present octagonal font dating from the 15th century replaced a tub-font now in the churchyard near the lychgate and was in turn thrown out about 1849. In the 16th or 17th centuries the north transept was either altered or rebuilt to form a manorial pew.

The brick tower, built in 1635, was the major surviving section in a fire which destroyed most of the church in 1914. The rebuilding was completed by 1916, on the same foundations. All the furnishings have been installed since then, with some very pleasing woodwork, especially the carved pews. Outside, the church of St. Mary's, Wargrave, with its fine tower, stands in a very pleasant setting of mature trees and open parkland.

Following the river south-west, and passing over the delta of the river Loddon as it joins the Thames, one comes to another ancient crossing place and the beautiful village of Sonning, surely an 'ideal' Thames-side village. St. Andrew's church too fulfils the idealised conception of the 'village church' with its tower, aisles, chapels and porches, and a multiplicity of roofs, all flint and stone and tile, set in a spacious

Tower c. 1631, Wargrave, Berks.

churchyard.

Here there are mellow Tudor brick walls around and, hard by the gates, the Bull Hotel, once the site of a church hostelry. Once more this is a church close to the river and to a road leading to a bridge. Here was an early crossing place with a settlement on one side only, promoted by the rise in the land from the river and the marshiness of the opposite bank.

Sonning was distinguished by an episcopal manor in Saxon times, one of the five seats of the Bishop of Ramsbury. This was probably after 909 A.D. when the Winchester diocese was subdivided. In 1058 Ramsbury and Sherbourne were united, the episcopal seat being transferred to Old Sarum (later Salisbury) in 1075. Walter Scammell was consecrated Bishop here in 1284. Sonning remained in the Salisbury diocese until 1836 when it was transferred to Oxford. The palace was used as an occasional seat until the 16th century.

As at Cookham one must look to the likelihood of there having been a Saxon church. The earliest identifiable remains, of the late 12th century, are the south doorway (presumably not in its original position) and a short pillar, now against a column near the north door. The latter, with its spiral decoration, was found in the chancel wall in 1852 and was probably a pillar-piscina as at Upton. The decoration should be compared with that on the font at Mapledurham.

Monument, Sonning.

Brass of Sir Laurence Fyton d. 1434, Sonning.

79

Assuming that there was then only a chancel and nave, a north aisle and chapel was added in the mid 13th century as shown by the bases of the north arcade columns. A south aisle was added in the early 14th century, and a little later the chancel was extended to the east, with its lovely carved arch in the north wall. It is likely that a tower was built then, as the base of the existing tower tends to indicate.

Further work to the nave and north aisle in the 15th century was

Robert Wright heraldic monument, Sonning.

followed by the re-building of the tower in the early 16th century. The patchwork tower construction, as at Bisham, would probably have been plastered over. Thus a medley of materials was used including a number of early carved stones. It is possible that the tower was further repaired or altered prior to new bells being installed in 1640-1641. About 1620 the south aisle was extended eastwards.

At the west end of the nave, the rear columns are buried in the rear wall, and it has been suggested that the church once extended further westward. However, much of this is probably due to the 16th century construction of the spiral tower stair in the thickness of the eastern piers.

The chancel is unusually long, perhaps created by the needs of the Bishops and their retinues when in residence. Apparently there was another chapel still further to the east at one time.

In 1852 a major restoration was commenced under the architect, Woodyer. Galleries, screens and other furnishings were removed, the nave was re-roofed with the addition of a clerestory, and much stone restoration carried out, including the decorated canopy arch in the chancel. It may have formed a tomb, as at present, or an Easter Sepulchre or both.

Further restoration was carried out in the 1870's and since, including recent re-decoration in 1961 and 1966.

There is a host of splendid monuments of many different periods and qualities. There are several brasses in the chancel floor, including notably the large representation of a knight in armour, to Laurence Fyton, a Bailiff of Sonning, d. 1434; a strange fragment of a late 16th century tomb in the south chancel aisle with six mutilated figures; also nearby a wall-monument to Lady Litcott, d. 1630. There are others of the 17th century, including the monstrous Rich memorial in the tower, c. 1663, now the last resting place of old hassocks. In the north vestry is a good heraldic wall-plaque to Robert Wright dated 1605.

Passing over Sonning's 18th century brick bridge and by the mill, one reaches the main road to Caversham. Though clinging to its village origins, this is now a suburb of Reading, and although on the north bank, part of Berkshire. From early times dependence on Reading as the market town must have existed.

Caversham Bridge is the older of the two river crossings, and was preceded by an ancient ford. Not far from this, but up on a steep wooded bank overlooking the Thames is the church of St. Peter. Immediately below is the site of the 17th century mansion, Caversham

Arcading, St. Peter's, Caversham.

Court, and of earlier manors from Saxon times. The siting of the church was determined presumably by the manor.

The earliest survival is the elaborate Norman south doorway, built about 1162 when the church was given to Notley Abbey by Walter Gifford, Earl of Buckingham. It is probable that an earlier church existed to which the font bowl presumably belonged. This unique piece, now mounted on a modern Norman base, was recovered from the grounds of the Court last century; its curious shaping is so simple and distinctive that, unless recut, it bears no relationship to other font forms.

For a long while the church only comprised a nave and chancel; the north aisle was added in the late 15th century with an eastern chapel dedicated to St. Mary, which became the Brigham, and later Vanderstegen, chapel after 1538. This has a fine arcade into the chancel with panelled arches and angel capitals.

From the early 17th century at least, a wooden west tower existed; a windvane dated 1663 is now in the chancel. In 1878, a new tower was built together with the south aisle and south arcade, accompanied by general restoration work. In 1924-5 the chancel was extended eastward by Sir Ninian Comper; the side windows then created enhance a very pleasant altar setting. The south aisle was extended at the same time to form the south chapel, which has the late 13th century former chancel window for its east window. Sir Ninian also designed the delicate dark oak screens and choir stalls. There are several wall memorials of the 17th, 18th and 19th centuries. Over Caversham Bridge lies a triangle of land bounded on two sides by the Rivers Thames and Kennet and forming a natural defensive site. Early man settled here; later, the Romans came, to be followed by Reada's people (Reading) in the Saxon occupation. Thus Reading came into existence.

The established town is first recorded in 871 A.D. when it was captured and held by the Danish raiders. The West Saxons, under Alfred, failed to dislodge them and had to buy peace; the Danes later withdrew to London. Reading was attacked and destroyed in the Danish incursions of 1006 when Wallingford also was ravaged. It was a very small township by modern standards. Domesday records just thirty houses, four mills and a church. However, as would seem the general pattern, the survey omitted much, especially minor dwellings and chapels, but recorded those principal buildings and estates which would bear taxation.

The church was almost certainly that to St. Mary the Virgin; this is still known as the Minster, a Saxon term for a monasterium (not a monastery), a church where a number of clergy led a communal life serving the parish and its satellite chapels. This would have been well established by 979 A.D. when, it would seem Queen Elfrida caused a convent to be erected alongside, 'at the ancient crossroads, near the ford of the Kennet'. All evidence of these early buildings has disappeared in the successive reconstructions. Now the earliest remain is a plain early Norman archway rebuilt into the north aisle wall as access to the War Memorial Chapel erected in 1918.

About 1200 the south arcade and aisle were built; the circular columns, with very stylised leaf capitals, belong to the Transitional period. The round-headed arches are curiously wide and flat, not true arcs, and it has been suggested that this arcade material was brought from the ruins of Reading Abbey in the 1550-3 restoration. However, Leyland in his survey for Henry VIII c. 1538, records St. Mary's as comprising a small north aisle, chancel, nave and south aisle. Also later records mentioned that there was a round-headed chancel arch until 1864, which would have been an improbable insertion in the mid 16th century. Also the insertion of an early arcade in place of another seems unlikely, but there could have been a major reconstruction in which the arches were stretched to cover an extended length. It is known that

St. Mary's, Reading.

84

the fine roof timbers came from the abbey, and that the splendid chequered flint and stone west tower was erected at the same time, 1550-3. Leland's 'north aisle' is the north transept chapel, c. 1300, to which was added the north aisle proper in 1872. In 1372 the existence of the Colney chantry chapel on the south side is recorded but its position is unknown.

The chancel was reconstructed and enlarged in 1864, with the addition of a south choir aisle, now the Lady Chapel. In the process, early English work of the 13th century was discovered and restored; this comprised windows, a piscina, credence and aumbry. Also restored is the double-arched recess on the north side of the sanctuary, perhaps an Easter Sepulchre although more like a tomb recess or even a sedilia. This is in the decorated style of the 14th century.

At the west end is the font, octagonal with quatrefoil panels, recorded as having been installed at the late date of 1616. Above is a good carved gallery erected in 1631 and extending one bay eastward at that time. It was moved back in 1864 when the organ was moved to the north transept. The tower was restored, 1921-9. Six years later the sanctuary was re-arranged and re-furnished.

The one major memorial is in the chancel, a large black and gilt wall monument to William Kendrick, d. 1635 who kneels facing his wife.

Outside, St. Mary's is very pleasingly set in an open tree-graced churchyard. Not quite so favoured but with an equally impressive tower is the church of St. Laurence, just a quarter of a mile away at the north end of the Market Place.

Midway along its southern flank once stood the outer west gate to Reading Abbey. Henry I founded this abbey in 1121 and many fine buildings were erected on an extensive site; the visible remains are now very fragmentary. Parts of the site have revealed early pagan burials. It seems that, being a place already hallowed in death, Christian interment followed, and that a small church stood here, perhaps in Saxon times, certainly in the early Norman period before the abbey was founded.

That church, a dependent of the minster in all probability, comprised a nave (of which the existing south wall survives) extending from the present chancel arch to the south door; immediately west of this the lower wall is thicker and may indicate the former presence of a west tower though it would have had a base area of exceptional size. All evidence of the early chancel has disappeared.

The abbey was endowed with many properties including Reading's

St. Laurence, Reading.

John Blagrove Memorial c. 1611.

churches: the earliest references are to St. Mary's in 1129, and to St. Laurence's and St. Giles', 1189-93. At that latter time St. Laurence's was granted to the newly-founded Hospitium of St. John built just to the north of the church, and of which later parts still stand. About

1196 the church was altered by the re-building of the chancel and the extension of the nave westward. It is not clear whether a tower was erected on the site of the present one at that time or later. Twenty years or so after, the north chapel to St. John was added – presumably for the particular use of the hospitium – together with a north aisle. The arcade between chancel and chapel has stiff-leaf capitals, a little more advanced than those at St. Mary's.

About 1450 many windows were altered, the north aisle arcade was rebuilt, and the tower reconstructed in its present imposing form with its flint and stone chequerwork and polygonal buttresses. This is the earliest example of this style of tower in the area covered by the survey; there are several later versions not necessarily drawing on St. Laurence's for inspiration for the style was in wide use. The north aisle appears to have been extended alongside the tower at this time, evidence the north arch inside; the lofty eastern arch into the nave is particularly fine.

Between 1520 and 1522 the nave was re-roofed and the arcade raised in height. Also installed at this time was the font, a simple panelled octagon, finely re-decorated in the medieval manner.

A great rood and loft was destroyed in 1562; the present rood screen was erected in 1922.

On the southern side, near where the abbey gate stood, a family chapel was built for Sir Francis Knollys in 1637; this was demolished last century, together with an arcade called Blagrave's Piazza, erected 1619-20. This was named after John Blagrave, the mathematician, d. 1611, whose interesting monument with half-effigy is on the south wall of the nave.

There are many other memorials of note including a palimpsest brass, in St. John's chapel, which is hung so that both sides can be examined. This is to Walter Barton, d. 1538, with the reverse to a knight, John Popham, d. 1463. In the north aisle is a small wall monument, with diminutive kneeling figures, to Thomas Lydall, d. 1608. Slightly later, 1636, is the kneeling figure of Martha Hamley, near the font. Yet another in the same posture is Ann Haydon, d. 1747, whose classical monument is in the chancel. Above the doorway to the tower stair and under a tall arch is a large standing figure of Dr. Valpy who died in 1838.

Surviving furnishings from before the 19th century restorations include three 15th century carved bench ends in the chancel; the organ case and keyboard of 1741, at the entrance to St. John's chapel (the

Martha Hamley d. 1636.

Font, St. Laurence, Reading.

90

organ is now at the west end of the aisle); and the 18th century pulpit with inlay work. Restoration work took place in 1848, 1867 and 1881; also following bomb damage in 1943.

St. Giles' church was outside the original town, just over the River Kennet and on the road from St. Mary's. The earliest indications are of a church built soon after the Conquest, probably a small chapel. This passed into the possession of the abbey, 1189-93. The development has been obscured by more recent work, but it would seem that in the late 13th century north and south aisles were added. A tower may well have existed by then, although it belongs principally to the 15th century. Several fragmentary pieces of stone-carving may be seen preserved on the south wall inside the tower and include a notable large capital, c. 1130. This could have come from the abbey ruins at a later date, as has been suggested; if not, it suggests a more developed early building, under the influence of the abbey. In 1872, St. Giles' was largely rebuilt by J. P. St. Aubyn, being extended on the east by á new elaborately decorated chancel, with Lady chapel, vestries and transepts. Further embellishment and re-decoration of the interior took place earlier this century, and again in 1949 and 1966.

The earliest memorial is a brass of 1521; there are many other memorials including an interesting and varied group from the 18th century.

The dominant external feature is the spire, almost too large for its tower. An early one was destroyed in 1643; a late 17th or early 18th century octagonal turret and spire, together with the top storey, was replaced in the 19th century reconstruction.

On the same route, but in the Caversham direction from St. Mary's is Reading's fourth medieval church, Greyfriars. As its name suggests, this was a special foundation established in 1285, for the Franciscan friars. They had arrived in Reading fifty-two years earlier but could only obtain from the abbey a very marshy site near the Thames where they built a wooden church and ancillary buildings. Because it proved so unsatisfactory a site, they were eventually granted the present one.

By about 1311, a wonderfully spacious church with nave, aisles, choir and chancel and possibly transepts, had been raised in the early English style. Apart from the choir and chancel, it is essentially that building which one sees today and which was carefully reconstructed by Woodman in 1863. This was necessary because, following the surrender of the friary to the Crown in 1538, and the fairly immediate destruction of choir and chancel, the remainder served as the Guildhall, then as a workhouse, house of correction, borough bride-well and county prison. By the mid 19th century the building was in a dreadful condition, but the Reverend W. Phelps, recognising its potential as a new church and its architectural worth, organised its purchase and through a public appeal raised the funds for the restoration which resulted in its reconsecration in December, 1863. The choir and chancel were not rebuilt, the sanctuary being placed against the closed-up eastern arch. A new parish was formed from parts of St. Laurence's and St. Mary's territories. Early in 1973 an interesting semi-circular suite of rooms was completed as a west extension.

CHAPTER VIII

Reading to Goring

In what has become part of the western suburb of Reading is the former village of Tilehurst. In 1291 it was described as a hamlet of Reading indicating its long-standing dependence on the market town. As a place it had its origins in tile-making on this formerly wooded hill, overlooking the Thames, shown in both the present name and the Old English 'Tygelhyrst'.

The first church may not have been built until Norman times; the first documentary reference is in a charter of Reading Abbey, c. 1189-93; the first architectural evidence is the early 14th century south aisle. The tower was rebuilt in its present brick form in 1737 and the rest of the present church, with its large gloomy interior and high pitched roof, was rebuilt by G. E. Street in 1856, with the addition of the spire to the tower.

There are two memorials of interest: brasses to Gavin More and his wife Isabella who both died in 1479 and, dominating the south aisle, the impressive and finely executed recessed tomb with its recumbent and praying effigies of Sir Peter Vanlore, d. 1627, and his wife, with children kneeling around.

A painting on the west wall indicates how St. Michael's church looked before 1856, with a Gothic Revival chancel arch and box-pews.

Between Tilehurst and Purley is a suburban continuation of Reading. There has been a considerable population growth in Purley parish in recent times, but the church of St. Mary the Virgin is at one edge, in Purley Park, close to the river where for many centuries there was a ferry providing a link with Mapledurham.

Probably in "Porlei", of the 11th century, the lord of the manor established a church or chapel for himself, his servants and tenants. The round-headed arch on the north side of the chancel is, apparently, the chancel arch of that original 11th century church. The font, with its near-cylindrical stone bowl with interlaced blank arcading, belongs

Monument to Sir Peter Vanlore d. 1627.

to the mid 12th century. On the east side of the bowl the arcading contains a head.

Only fragments survive of later development, the church being largely rebuilt in 1870. The pleasing west tower, of red brick with stone dressings and grotesque gargoyles, is dated 1626. However, the inside is of rough stone suggesting that this is essentially an earlier tower.

There are good examples of 17th, 18th and 19th century monuments including one in the tower to Ann Hyde, who died in 1632 aged 20; she is shown lying on her side with her baby.

Over the river is Mapledurham House, the great Tudor brick home of the Blount family. Sir Richard, who died in 1628, and his wife Cicely, d. 1618, are commemorated in effigy in St. Margaret's church which stands by the gates of the house. This church probably began with the Norman manor though the place was settled earlier as the Old English origin of Mapledurham – the settlement by the maple trees — suggests.

In the first half of the 12th century the existing font was made, a large cylinder with diagonally cut banding. Between 1254 and 1289 the church was rebuilt, perhaps with the addition of the tower. Sir Robert Bardolf added the south aisle, 1380-95; he died in the latter year and his brass memorial is in that aisle which is still the private chapel of the successive Roman Catholic owners of the manor. The Bardolf's house was rebuilt by the Blounts in the 16th century.

Blount effigies, Mapledurham.

In 1862-3 the church was restored by William Butterfield who added the unusual north aisle with its oak pillars and raised the height of the tower. When re-roofing the chancel, the panelled and decorated early 16th century roof was fortunately retained; the 18th century pulpit was removed however. The 19th century marble reredos has now been covered by curtaining which greatly simplifies the altar setting. In the east window are some old fragments of stained glass, and three good panels of European origin.

Close to the church is an ancient mill and the tiny village with its pleasing variety of buildings. It is now remote from the main road, but an early trackway once passed through here from Caversham to Whitchurch, continuing up the river. This is now a bridleway passing through the lovely Hardwick estate on to a road which joins the single long street of Whitchurch at its head.

Down past the many fine old buildings one comes to the iron toll-bridge of 1891. The first bridge was erected in 1793, prior to which there was a ferry.

From the bridge one can see the mill pool in all its beauty, and, for the first time, the small shingled spire of the church of St. Mary the Virgin. Once found, tucked away behind the surrounding houses, it is an attractive small church of stone and flint, largely rebuilt in 1858 by Woodyer.

The main entrance is by the north door, but far more interesting is the lovely early 16th century south porch with its moulded entrance arch flanked by shield-bearing angels and surmounted by a crucifix panel, the cross with leaves like a tree, the figure now decayed.

Inside is a Norman doorway, with a pair of early leaf capitals on one side only. Within the arch has been set a later doorway contemporary with the porch. Above is an extraordinary grotesque face, quite possibly of the early 11th century, a fragment of the Saxon church here indicated by the Old English 'Witcerc', white church, perhaps built of chalk rubble, plastered and limewashed. As Hwitcurke it is first recorded in 1012 when the manor was granted to Abingdon Abbey.

The interior is all of the 19th and early 20th centuries. The chancel arch is unfortunately heavy in appearance, but the furnishings are simple and well-ordered. It is said that the north aisle occupies the site of two medieval chapels.

There are numerous memorials, the earliest being the four brasses. Two are of good quality: that to Thomas Walysch, dressed in knightly armour, with his wife, c. 1420, who held the manor from the Crown

96

St. Mary's, Whitchurch.

and was trayer (taster of wines) to John of Gaunt and Henry IV, Henry V and Henry VI; and that of a vested priest, Roger Gery, who died in 1484 although the date is not completed in the inscription.

The earliest monument is in the chancel, a Renaissance style memorial, with kneeling effigies of Sir Richard Lybbe of Hardwicke and his wife Joanna, both of whom died in 1599. Also in the chancel, to the south of the altar, is a single light window with late 15th or early 16th century stained glass. The figure — variously described as a bishop with crozier, possibly St. Birinus - is in fact an Archbishop of Canterbury in full pontificals, denoted by the pallium, the sign of papal authority, worn over the chasuble. The halo normally denotes a saint so this would in all probability be a retrospective depiction of either St. Edmund of Abingdon, Archbishop of Canterbury 1234-45, or St. Thomas à Becket, Archbishop of Canterbury 1162-74. Whitchurch remains a residential village, with its commercial centre in Pangbourne, over the toll-bridge.

11th century carving over South Door, Whitchurch.

Brass of Thomas Walysch c. 1420.

Pangbourne was a Saxon settlement by a tributary of the Thames referred to in the name as the stream of Paega's folk. At a crossroads in the village is the church of St. James the Less with its distinctive brick tower of 1718. As with Tilehurst, the rest was rebuilt in the 19th century, this time by Woodman in 1866-8, and is a good example of an interior of that period. There is a Jacobean pulpit, a number of hatchments, a few memorials and particularly the large, grey and much-mutilated monument, hidden behind the organ, to Sir John Davis who died in 1625. Above the south doorway is a carved and decorated Royal Coat of Arms of George II.

The living was in the gift of Reading Abbey in the late 12th century, so that the existence of a Norman church can be assumed.

The road and railway west out of Pangbourne hug the river as the hills drop steeply to the valley at this point. Further on, the river sweeps away around a long bend enclosing a level alluvial meadow. Here an ancient trackway crossed the river; this became a Roman road and ford with a substantial villa close by. The ford evidently continued in use, witness the 7th and 9th century name, Bestlesford.

From the 11th century the place name was Bastledene, Bestlesden, Beselden and so on to today's Basildon. Possibly use of the ford declined or the river level rose making crossing difficult, but a ferry existed until early this century.

Essentially this has remained a manor farm, with manorial church with little cause for growth. Today, with a growing population and new church at Upper Basildon, St. Bartholomew's church is no longer used and likely to be declared redundant; already the very plain interior is in a state of neglect.

Of the 11th century church there is no trace; it was given to the Abbey of Lire, in Normandy, before 1154, but returned to the Crown in 1337. The church one sees now is primarily of the late 13th century and was hardly altered, it would seem, except for the 15th century roofs and the addition of the brick west tower in 1734, until the major restoration of 1875-6.

The few items of interest are a Perpendicular font of standard form; a brass in the nave floor, to John Clerk, d. 1497, and his wife Lucy, and outside, on the south chancel wall, an ornate but crumbling 14th century tomb canopy which was moved here to form a memorial to Sir Francis Sykes, who died in 1804. Nearby is a recent memorial stone to Jethro Tull, 1674-1740, the pioneer of mechanized agriculture.

Upstream is one of the early major crossing places where the river

100

cuts through the chalk ridge forming Goring Gap. The ridge was a natural highway, recalled in the Ridgeway and the Icknield Way; the ford attracted settlement at a very early date and remains of the Neolithic period have been found. At some stage the crossing was improved by a causeway, presumably with a draw-bridge in the centre. By the medieval period the route was no longer as important, and a ferry operated by the Prioress of Goring was adequate, for a bridge was not built until 1838.

On the south side is Streatley, recorded as early as the 7th century as Streatlea – the glade by the (Roman) road – and in the 9th century as Estralei.

The church, St. Mary's is close to the river and to the crossing, as is Goring church opposite. Apart from the 15th century west tower, the rest is of 1865 when the church was rebuilt on the same lines, it is said, as the previous 13th century building. No early remains exist, but records indicate that there was a church in 1086. From 1255 it belonged to Hurley Priory until the dissolution of that priory. Memorials include a brass of 1440.

On the north bank is Goring, the place of Gara's people. Alongside the mill stream is the church of St. Thomas of Canterbury. From the bridge the impressive tower with its remarkable Norman stair-turret can be seen to good advantage. This was probably built in the first half of the 12th century – together with the nave and an eastern apse on the lines of the present one – for the Augustinian nunnery founded here under a grant of Henry I, 1100-1135. It is reasonable to suppose that it replaced an earlier Norman or late Saxon building.

The tall nave has windows set high because of the ancillary buildings including cloisters, originally around the outside. At the west end is the original tower arch and behind the modern studded leather doors is the monolithic circular font, quite plain except for heavy tooling which must belong to the time of its return to the church in 1937, having been removed in 1848. The tower floor here is lower and probably represents the original level; above is a groined stone vault. The Norman west doorway is a somewhat unusual design with a roundel in the head, now enclosing a modern cross; the second doorway has angle columns with volute capitals. Also with similar capitals are the central balusters of the three twin-light tower windows. Above these are Perpendicular belfry windows and parapet.

In the early 13th century the south chapel aisle was constructed, the massive pillars and arches being inserted in the wall, so shortening the windows above.

Norman Tower, St. Thomas, Goring.

About 1300 the nuns built their own church by taking down the apse and building eastward, with a screen separating them from the parishioners. After the dissolution of the nunnery, their church was destroyed and the east end sealed off. The present apse was built in the late 19th century. The furnishings also date from then or from early this century, including the rood screen of 1910. Of the five brasses, the best is that with an effigy and parts of a canopy to Elizabeth Loveday who died in 1401.

On the vestry wall are many 13th and 14th century floor tiles with a variety of designs. Above the tower arch is a bell cast by Richard de Wymbis about 1290.

CHAPTER X

Goring to Wallingford

From Goring a minor road, fading into a bridletrack leads northwards between river and railway to South Stoke. This track, and the paths through Little Stoke Manor, North Stoke, Mongewell, and Newnham Farm to Wallingford bridge may well represent an old road, before the present B4009.

South Stoke could have arisen as a minor crossroad settlement, the road being crossed by a route from the east over the river to Moulsford and the Downs.

The name Stoke, from the Old English 'stoc', is difficult to interpret for this place, as there are several possible meanings, the most probable is cattle or dairy farm.

In the centre of the old village stands St. Andrews church, the walls refreshingly limewashed as were so many of our lesser churches until the 19th century. In contrast the interior is dark, only lit by the low aisle windows to north and south. However, it too has been recently whitened, and the chancel is especially resplendent with re-decorated ceilings and monuments, and a pleasingly simple altar arrangement.

Either side of the east window are two fine plaques, identical cartouches, to Elizabeth Barber, d. 1657, and Richard Hannes, d. 1678. Close by, on the north wall, is a more delicate tablet to Lucy Harward, d. 1718, and her mother, d. 1728. Nearer the chancel arch is a splendid wall monument with a clerical half-effigy presiding over a vast verbose dedication; this commemorates Dr. Griffith Higgs who died in 1659 having been chaplain to Elizabeth, Queen of Bohemia and daughter of James I of England.

Whatever early church was here disappeared in the major reconstructions of the 13th and 14th centuries. In the Early English style of the mid 13th century are the lancet windows at the east and west ends of both aisles and the circular-columned north arcade. It would seem that the octagonal-columned south arcade was rebuilt during the restoration work of 1857. The east window and probably the chancel arch are in the Decorated style of the early 14th century. The two canopied image niches in the aisles probably date from the end of the 16th century. Also 14th century is the simple octagonal font.

By that time the church comprised chancel, nave, aisles and west tower; the latter was partially rebuilt in the 15th century. In the centuries since, only minor alterations have occurred such as the building of the south porch during the 19th century restorations.

Not so many years ago there was a ferry across to the Betel and Wedge Inn at Moulsford. Centuries before that there was a ford, recalled in the village name and situated perhaps by the little church, a short distance upstream.

Attractively set on higher ground only a little distance from the river bank, St. John the Baptist's church would seem to have been provided as much for travellers as for villagers, being at the intersection of a river crossing, an ancient road, and a Roman road from the west. Also, any fording place would have been a natural site for baptism during the period of the Saxon conversion. In this context the dedication is particularly appropriate.

A chapel here was first recorded about 1220-7 when it belonged to Wallingford Priory, but it is believed that it was built about 1100 by a Norman patron. Although the church was rebuilt in 1846, the retention of the rubble west wall indicates that it is much the same size as it always was. The tiny north aisle could be a medieval addition, for it would be hard to attribute the quaint arcade to the restorer, Sir G. G. Scott, or to any later architect.

The mother church of the Moulsford chapel, until its 19th century restoration, was St. Mary's, Cholsey, two miles to the north and on the open level hinterland.

This was Ceol's island (Ceolesig in 891 A.D.), probably a dry place in a marshy area. Here was founded a monastery in the Saxon period, apparently close to where the railway station now stands and about half-a-mile away from the church which is in an isolated position by Manor Farm.

It seems likely that the monastery, a small one, was destroyed during the Danish attacks of 1006; the community was apparently disbanded unless it continued to serve the new church.

Manor Farm probably represents the Saxon manor, evidently a place of considerable wealth and patronage for seemingly it established a substantial church in the early 11th century. The clues to this are to be found in the central tower: on the north east angle in particular, just

12th Century Doorway, Cholsey, Berks.

above the roof line, is an adequate example of long and short quoining, an identifiable characteristic of Saxon work. It only continues for a few courses because the upper part of the tower was reconstructed in the late 14th century when the stair turret was added.

After the Conquest, possession passed to the Abbey of Mont St. Michael in Normandy. Between 1125 and 1129 it was transferred to the newly-formed abbey at Reading. It was the latter's great barn which until 1815 stood close by. It was the largest known, at 303 feet long. About 1150-1160 a major rebuilding took place resulting in a cruciform church with a shorter chancel, almost certainly terminating in an eastern apse; two transepts, each with an eastern apse, indicated by the blocked arch in the north transept and the discovery of foundations on the south side; and a nave, about thirteen feet shorter than at present. The church, with its chapels, tends to indicate the existence of a sub-community of the abbey, a conjecture which could be confirmed by the extension of the east end and a little over one hundred years later, creating the spacious abbey-style chancel with its large early English windows.

The entrance to the church is by a fine Norman south doorway, c. 1160, until 1849 a porch protected it. Just to the west is a re-discovered narrow Norman window, now glazed, but still blocked inside. Inside the simple whitened nave there is a great calm; overall is a pleasing timbered roof of 1849. The west end, with its colourful window, was a late 15th century extension. To the east is the comparatively small tower arch leading under the great tower, passing four exceptionally fine, albeit restored, late Norman carved capitals, into the lovely chancel. Tall, elegant triple-lancet windows enhance each side of the sanctuary; at the base of those on the south are sedilia and a piscina. Either side of the crossing, through massive round-headed arches are the transepts; the chapel to the south has a south window, c. 1300, when that whole wall was apparently rebuilt; the transept vestry to the north had its north wall rebuilt in 1877-8 when a general restoration took place. Also in that transept is a vast Tyrolean dresser, c. 1700.

There are few monuments; in the south transept is a mutilated early 14th century stone effigy, perhaps of an abbess of prioress, again indicative of a religious community here; there are fragments and matrices of brasses, the earliest to John Barfoot who died in 1361.

Another church dedicated to St. Mary is at North Stoke on the Oxfordshire bank of the Thames, a small quiet village which began perhaps as a cattle or dairy farm in Saxon times. This seems the most

Effigy of an abbess, Cholsey.

appropriate interpretation of 'stoc', although the use of the word to denote the cell of a hermit or other holy place cannot be ruled out; a confusing factor is the existence of South Stoke, one and three quarters of a mile away with Little Stoke Manor in between.

There is no evidence of a Saxon church here; a preaching cross would probably have sufficed. Nor is there any real evidence of a Norman church being built soon after the Conquest. The earliest indication is given by the fragmentary remains of a short pillar, perhaps a pillar piscina, c. 1160. Whatever else existed was obliterated by the church built in the mid 13th century, comprising the present chancel and nave, and the base of the tower. The latter partially collapsed in 1669, was repaired, and then completed in its present form with red brick detailing in 1726.

Dating from the mid 13th century are the pleasing clustered columns with carved capitals of the chancel arch, and the simple font.

About 1300 the walls were elaborately painted with scenes from the lives of Christ and the saints, including, on the north chancel wall, a portrayal of the murder of St. Thomas à Becket. Much painting is still in evidence and can be identified with study and with the aid of the notes available in the church.

The timbered south porch, though partly reconstructed, contains a very old portal frame.

Only minor alterations and additions have been made since (excepting the tower) so that on entering the church the impression is one of great antiquity, a combination of ancient woodwork and stone, brick and tiled floors, and faded images. There are 14th century tiles; a fragment of a brass to Roger Parkers, sometime rector and a Canon of St. George's chapel, Windsor, who died in 1363; an oak pulpit with backboard and canopy with low relief carving typical of the early 17th century; and outside, above the blocked south doorway, a remarkable sundial with a head above and hands holding the roundel. The arms were apparently found during the general restoration of 1902, and covered up again; but the head seems out of proportion and character and rather like a corbel head which has been 'assembled' with the dial. This is difficult to date but could belong to the major rebuilding period of the mid 13th century; the head could be contemporary.

A bridleway from North Stoke takes one to Mongewell Park, now the grounds of Carmel College. Here, on a low wooded rise by the river and lapped by an ornamental lake, stand the forlorn ruins of St. John the Baptist's church.

St. Mary's, North Stoke.

110

The spring feeding the 'lake' was probably the 'well' of the Mund-ingas, denoting settlement here in the Saxon period.

From the restored remains of the apse and chancel, which are weathertight and used for summer Sunday evening services, it can be seen that a well-built Norman church existed. The nave, with later alterations, is roofless and overgrown. At the west end is a curious brick tower with a circular base and hexagonal upper storeys, probably added in the early 19th century.

Less than half-a-mile to the north, and reached by continuing along the bridlepath, is another remote and dis-used church, dedicated to St. Mary the Virgin. This small, plain building would have only Newnham Murren farm to serve, thus it has been used for some years and is likely to be officially declared redundant. The first church was evidently built to serve a manor farm and its estate tenants soon after the Conquest; and that has been its continuing purpose so long as the estate was prosperous and well-populated. That has all changed.

The original church comprised the present tall nave, with its high chancel arch, and a small chancel. About 1250 the latter was extended eastward with a new east window, and the somewhat unusual circular font was installed. About this time Sir Richard Morin was lord of the manor, and Murren is derived from his name.

A south aisle was added later, with an odd squint through to the chancel. Little else changed over the centuries until the 1848 restoration when the south aisle was rebuilt and a new bell-cote added.

The hexagonal pulpit is a rich example of the late Jacobean or early Caroline style, with carved strapwork decoration.

The village of Newnham Murren now borders the south side of the road to Wallingford bridge, with Crowmarsh Gifford and its church of St. Mary Magdalene on the opposite side, for originally this was all part of the parish of Newnham. St. Mary's was not at first a parish church, but was founded about 1120 to serve as a chapel to a leper hospital belonging to Wallingford. Seemingly the 'crow marsh' was the right place to which to despatch the unfortunate sufferers. Only after the Reformation was the chapel given a parish with a vicar; in 1672 this became a rectory.

The patched and weather-worn walls of this simple church belie the high quality of that first building which has survived remarkably well. Being a chapel, especially to a leper hospital, there was not the patronage or religious and social pressures to effect great changes. So it has remained a basic nave and square-ended chancel, only extended by

Mass Dial, St. Mary's, North Stoke.

West Door, St. Mary Magdalene, Crowmarsh Gifford.

a north chapel in the early 13th century.

The Norman south door, the main entrance for many centuries, is now blocked; the outline of a porch can still be seen. Likewise the finely carved west doorway was also blocked, but was re-opened in 1839. Apart from a central single light above there are also two unusual small windows in this west wall.

Just inside is the font, described as Norman. It is rather smaller than most of its contemporaries suggesting a late date; the arcading, though a common motif of late work is not typical; and overall its regularity and crispness seem to owe a great deal to the 19th century restorers. The base is said to belong to the restoration but the unusual choice of a triple clustered pillar suggests the possibility of its being original, in which case it would tend to confirm a very late date, c. 1200. This could account for the debased style of decoration, quite unlike the earlier carving elsewhere in the church. This is at its best around the east window, and the splendid triple light in the south chancel wall; the capitals have basketwork or quasi-classical detailing. These, together with the west doorway, and the fine example of a piscina with projecting bowl, date from about 1160-80.

The north chapel, with its arch and windows, and the window in the north chancel wall belong to the early English style, c. 1230. A large window was inserted in the south wall of the nave in the early 15th century.

About 1836 there was a major restoration at the expense of William Seymour Blackstone, member of Parliament for Wallingford from 1832 to 1852. At that time the two blank arcades in the east wall were made; and the furnishings were completely altered for no early items remain. The pulpit, though of the 17th century, was given to the church about 1900. The present furnishings date mostly from the late 19th and early 20th centuries. The memorials, including a late 16th century brass, are of limited interest.

WALLINGFORD   Of a similar age and interest is the church of St. Leonard's in Wallingford across the river. It stands close to the river, little more than four hundred yards from the bridge, by a brook; perhaps this was a place of baptism for the church originated in Saxon times and could have been the first in Wallingford. It would have been destroyed with the town in the Danish attack of 1006, but as the town mint was soon working again one may assume that rebuilding was quickly carried out on town and church alike. The early 11th century building could be represented by the present nave and chancel, extensively altered in the middle of the 12th century by the addition of the eastern apse, and the construction of the wide carved arches to the chancel and apse. These are notable examples displaying a variety of geometric ornament, basket-work and two heads. The north doorway is also of this period. A south aisle was added, probably in the following century.

In 1646, during the siege of the castle in the Civil War, Cromwell's soldiers used the church as a barracks and caused great destruction. It was partially repaired in 1656, with further work in 1695 and 1700. Finally, in 1849-1850, extensive restoration was carried out which involved the building of the present apse, on the old foundations; the rebuilding of the south aisle, and the erection of the singularly inappropriate west tower, all to the designs of Hakewill.

Behind the 17th century Town Hall in the market place, rises the sturdy, pinnacled tower of St. Mary-le-More. This dates from 1653, the earlier tower having been damaged in a storm a number of years before; some older materials, including stone from the castle, were used but parts of the original tower may well be incorporated. A figure of a horseman may represent Richard, Earl of Cornwall, who could have been a benefactor; certainly he was responsible for the expenditure of 10,000 marks on the improvement of the castle in the mid 12th century. The pinnacles were added in 1660 but replaced with copies in glass-reinforced resin in 1964. The rest of the church was reconstructed in 1854 under the direction of David Brandon, the north vestry was converted to a chapel in 1911, the former chapel is now the vestry. There is over-ornate marble work of 1901 in the sanctuary, a marble pulpit with bronze figures of 1888, and an elaborate rood erected in 1925.

In the chancel are wall monuments of the 18th and 19th century. In the south aisle is a large well-detailed example commemorating Walter Bigg who died in 1659.

It seems likely that a church was built here in the late 11th century, arising perhaps from a re-structuring of the town for it is probable that a bridge was built in the present position at that period (first documentary evidence 1141). This was a very important crossing, known as from the 9th century, as Waelingford (the ford of Wealh's people) with defensive works, dating from ancient times, which had been reinforced during the Danish invasions. Before the Conquest it was a royal borough; Wigod, its lord in 1066, favoured William's cause, and so it came about that the Conqueror's army forded the Thames

115

St. Mary le More, Wallingford.

here. Subsequently William had a castle built to control this important point, as part of his overall network of defences which included castles at Oxford and Windsor. Until 1416, when Abingdon bridge was built, this was the major east-west route. Up till then the town's prosperity had been sufficient to support eleven churches, three chapels of religious orders, and one bridge chapel. These rapidly declined to just four churches, one of which was totally destroyed in the Civil War. Of the three remaining today, St. Mary's and St. Leonard's are both parish churches, but serving a united parish; St. Peter's, hard by the bridge, has been declared redundant and is closed for public worship. Its origins are obscure but it could have started as a bridge chapel in the late 11th century or early 12th century. The present apsidal east end, built in 1904, may or may not reflect an earlier plan, for the whole church was reconstructed between 1760 and 1769, having been in a state of disrepair from the time of the Civil War. In 1777 it was crowned with Sir Robert Taylor's delightful open spire which is such a fine feature of the river scene.

CHAPTER X

Wallingford to Abingdon

If Wallingford has a long and important history, Benson, to the
north on the Oxford bank, has an even older one for it was a British
settlement at a ford subsequently used by the Romans. It became the
centre of a West Saxon tribe, Bensington, the 'tun' of Benesa's people.
Here, Offa, King of Mercia, defeated the West Saxon armies in 779
A.D. and annexed this northern bank of the Thames. As a royal manor
it passed to the successive monarchs of England; its many possessions
included the hamlets of Henley and Warborough at the time of
Domesday.

Offa is reputed to have erected a stone church dedicated to St.
Helena. It is to be supposed that rebuilding followed until about 1140
when the Empress Matilda gave the church, with that at Warborough,
to endow Dorchester Abbey.

Thirty years or so later the chancel and nave were probably extended
and certainly altered with new windows, three of which still survive in
the chancel. Contemporary with these is the simple stone tub-font,
which has a 17th century wooden cover.

A lancet window at the east end of the south aisle was formerly in
the north aisle until 1862; dating from about 1200, it may have
indicated the presence of a north transeptal chapel. Not long after,
extensive alterations resulted in the chancel arch, aisles and arcades
being built. Three arcade capitals have stiff-leaf carving which is more
advanced than that at St. Laurence's, Reading, and probably contemporary with that at Long Wittenham, 1230-50. About a hundred
years later a new east window was inserted, together with the surviving
aisle windows and south doorway.

In the late 15th or early 16th century the aisle and nave roofs were
replaced with ones of lower pitch. Inside, the main oak beams have
carved bosses in the aisles and carved corbels in the nave. The cleres-

St. Helena's, Benson, Oxon.

tory windows may not have been inserted until the 18th century when new galleries required light. This would have been after the demolition of the old west tower and the construction, in 1780-1, of the present attractive if idiosyncratic one with its pinnacled parapet.

Some alterations to the south aisle and the erection of the south porch took place in 1841; the 18th century furnishings were replaced by G. E. Street in 1853-4 and in 1861-2 a major restoration was carried out under Charles Backridge. In particular this involved the rebuilding of the chancel, but preserving three early single-light windows. Further alterations to furnishings have taken place since; the interior is at present being re-arranged to provide a nave altar for the main Sunday Eucharist, as at Bray.

Leaving Benson the main road continues north west with the river; passing the turn to Shillingford bridge, a road to the right leads to Warborough, half-a-mile inland. At the far end of the village is Town Hill, which would have been the watch hill, the Old English form of which gave rise to the name, Warborough.

Before the Conquest the small settlement here would probably have been served by the cathedral at Dorchester sending a priest to hold services in the open or in a house.

Roof detail, St. Helena's, Benson.

Warborough was owned by the royal manor of Benson; about 1140 the Crown, in the form of Empress Matilda, granted the chapel of Warborough to Dorchester Abbey. Of that building there are no remains. The oldest piece is the circular lead font which is identical in most of its detailing with that at Long Wittenham. Low-relief rosettes and 'sun' wheels, vertical panels and groups of four arches each containing a figure decorate the surface. These identical figures are of a mitred and vested priest with a cross, and hand raised in blessing. The use of a cross rather than a crozier, suggests he is an archbishop; the style of mitre indicates a date of 1220 or later. The stone base is a good example of panelled 15th century work.

Possibly this church of St. Laurence was rebuilt when it passed to the abbey, but it is only known for certain that much was altered in the first half of the 13th century from the east and south windows of the chancel, and the south chancel doorway, with its contemporary iron-work. These windows and others were altered again in the early 14th century, when the south chapel was added. Also the long nave may have been extended westward and a tower erected. Several windows were changed in the following century.

In 1638 a west gallery was erected and the dormer windows inserted to light it. The upper part of the screen may belong to this period also. On the east side is an unusual 17th century depiction of the Prince of Wales' plume; the west side was very likely painted with the Royal Arms. The pulpit is also of this period, though restored. Evidently the church suffered during the Civil War and Commonwealth for it was described as 'ruinous'. The very substantial tower – in general form similar to that at Dorchester – was erected in 1666, the date being boldly shown on the west face; but it took until about 1675 for the rest to be put in order.

A major restoration took place in 1912-14 and most of the furnishings and arrangements are of that period. The fine nave roof was opened up then, and has since been attractively lit to reveal its pleasing structure. A wall-painting on the nave north wall, discovered in 1902 and thought to be a 13th century depiction of St. George and the Dragon, has now decayed beyond all recognition.

DORCHESTER. From Warborough it is only a short distance to the river Thame winding its way to join the Thames. Over the long causeway towering above the willows, is the great abbey church of St. Peter and St. Paul, the cathedral site of the Saxon diocese of Dorchester, established by St. Birinus in 635 A.D.

121

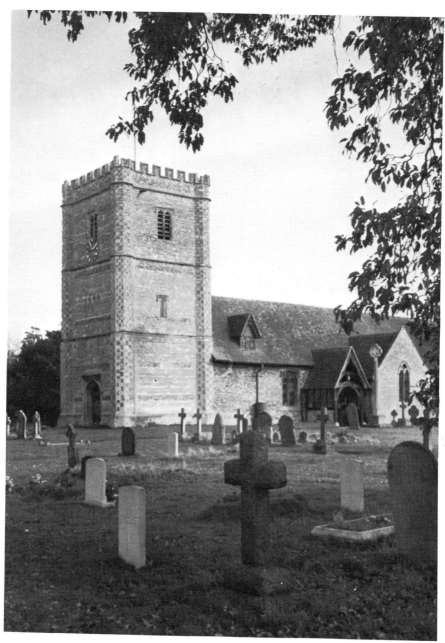

St. Laurence's, Warborough.

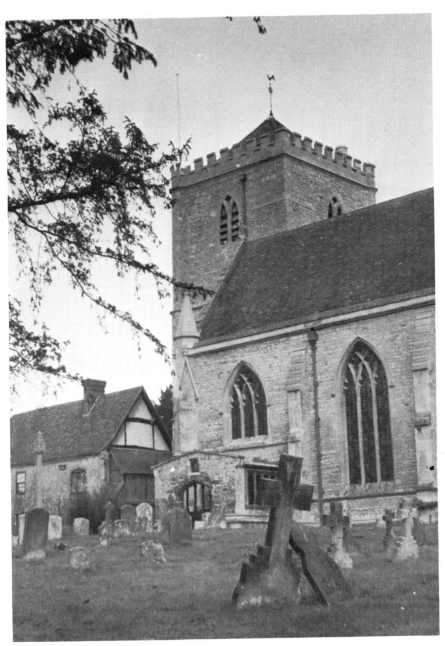

Abbey, Dorchester.

123

Dorchester seems to have been an important place from very early times, being close to the junction of two rivers – in fact guarded on three sides – and with routes to north and south. It became Dorocina, a Roman town, on the road between Alcester and Silchester, situated by the crossings of the Thame, and the Thames probably east of Little Wittenham Wood.

Of Birinus' cathedral we have no knowledge, but it may be reasonably assumed that by the late Saxon period a large stone building stood here, which the Normans rebuilt, most probably to a similar plan of nave, central tower, transepts and chancel apse. This was about 1120, by when the cathedral had been moved to Lincoln, and the church granted to an Augustinian community for its abbey.

The characteristic long and tall nave can still be gauged, though the later windows in the north wall and the elegant south arcade now reduce the effect. The south aisle was added by 1340 to serve as the parish church, the entrance being via the large 15th century porch. That is why the east wall presents a blank face, for it was the west wall of the Abbey Lady chapel. The blankness, however, was relieved by elaborate wall-paintings of which traces survive. Behind the raised altar is a particularly fine 14th century painting of the Crucifixion.

Sir John Holcomb d. 1310.

Once, screens between the arches would have separated the laity from the religious. On one column is a great corbel, perhaps intended as a base for statues, carved with sleeping monks. Close by is one of the treasures, a lead font of exceptional quality, c. 1150, with high relief representations of the Apostles set in arcading. By comparison, the lead fonts at Warborough and Long Wittenham are poor relatives.

In the nave, one's eye is caught by the sparkling web of stone tracery and coloured glass that is the great east window, with its massive central buttress. Much of the glass is of the 14th century, gathered together from other windows in the 18th century and restored in 1966. Below is the high altar in a spacious and dignified setting.

To the south is a superb 14th century sedilia with three seats and a piscina all under a richly carved canopy, and with unusual windows at the back containing 13th century stained glass panels representing scenes from the life of St. Birinus. Opposite is the unique Jesse window, its tracery forming a tree on which abound carved statues of prophets and kings, wise men and angels, and the broken remains of Christ and the Virgin and Child. The window, now mostly clear, contains some old glass.

This magnificent sanctuary was added about 1340, extending the Norman church eastward. Seventy years or so before, the north chancel aisle and chapel, now dedicated to St. Birinus, was built but not opened through into the chancel until later, perhaps because part served as a sacristy originally. A 13th century roundel of stained glass in the chapel east window depicts St. Birinus being commissioned by Pope Honorius I. The altar below is covered with a fine frontal designed by F. E. Howard in 1936. The west end of this aisle was rebuilt, in place of the north transept, in the early 17th century. After the north chapel but before the sanctuary, the Lady Chapel and aisle to the south were added to house the shrine of St. Birinus, fragments of the original being incorporated in its modern counterpart of 1964. The east end vaulting and gallery belong to the 19th century restoration but may have replaced original work.

During this great activity in the late 13th and 14th centuries it is likely that the central tower was demolished and a western tower built. This was rebuilt in 1605 but incorporating an earlier spiral staircase.

About 1870 onwards, careful restoration work was carried out under Sir G. G. Scott and W. Butterfield. Further extensive stone restoration outside was completed in 1970.

Both approaches to the church, whether from the bridge or from the town (passing under the imposing lychgate designed by Butterfield), converge on the south porch and the 14th century standing cross restored last century.

All the memorials of note are comparatively early, commencing with two Norman coffin slabs. Then, in the Lady Chapel aisle are three tombs: the superb knight, intensely alert and grasping his sword hilt, is an early alabaster carving, c. 1310, possibly representing the crusader Sir John Holcomb. By contrast, Sir John Seagrave's effigy is in serene, prayerful repose on a carved and buttressed 14th century tomb chest. The third is of John de Stonore, sometime Lord Chief Justice under Edward III. There is also another 14th century effigy, apparently representing a Saxon bishop.

Set in the floor all around are many brasses and matrices, notably the large mutilated figure of Sir John Drayton, d. 1417; the robed figure of Abbot Richard Bewforest, c. 1510; and Sir Richard Bewforest, d. 1512, and his wife.

Finally, it is as well to remember that its beginnings were as a cathedral, and its formative years were as an abbey; only after that was it solely a parish church.

One of the routes away from Roman Dorchester would seem to have been by fording the Thames in the vicinity of Day's Lock, skirting Wittenham Clumps near where a Roman altar was found in the 18th

Sir John Seagrave c. 1350.

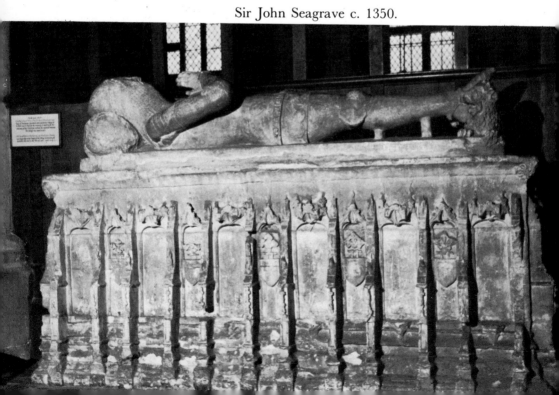

century, and so south-west to the Downs to join other routes. Today one can still cross by footpath and iron bridge, and be immediately confronted with the distinctive northern outcrop of the downs, which because of the commanding views for many miles around and oversight of a crossing place, was a very natural defensive site. On Castle Hill is a fort of older times, possibly the Iron Age. There was a Romano-British settlement here for about four hundred years until the coming of the Saxons in the 5th century. A Saxon homestead was established, probably nearer the ford. This was the beginning of Witta's settlement, still known as Witteham in the 13th century – later Wittenham. With the decline of Dorchester after the Conquest, presumably the use of the route also declined and with it the future of Wittenham. A neighbouring, more recent settlement with a mill grew to become West, Earl's, then Great Wittenham and eventually Long Wittenham, leaving Little Wittenham the hamlet it is today.

A church was recorded here in 1086, which may very well have been of Saxon foundation. The oldest part of St. Peter's church now is the lower part of the tower, from the 14th century the top dates from the following century. The rest of the building was entirely rebuilt in 1863, with a vestry and organ chamber being added in 1902.

A 15th century octagonal font of standard pattern has been preserved, together with a good and varied collection of monumedts. Against the north wall of the chancel is an altar tomb with cusped canopy arch, bearing a boldly cut brass of a man in civilian dress, Geoffrey Kidwelly, who died in 1483. Nearby, in the floor, is a larger well-delineated figure of his wife, Cecily, who died eleven years before. Another Kidwelly, David, d. 1454, is depicted on a smaller brass. Another of 1433 depicts John Churmond, priest.

At the west end are five later brasses, of characteristically poor quality, some with figures, others with shields or just inscriptions. That to William Dunche, who was Auditor of the Mints under Henry VIII and Edward VI, bears no date, but belongs to the mid-1580's. He is shown with his wife, Mary.

The west wall of the tower is occupied by the alabaster effigies of Sir William Dunch, d. 1611, and his wife, Mary, he reclining and she recumbent. Along the front of the base are their nine children. The figures are well carved and detailed, but the whole, without its canopy and colouring, is now poor in comparison with the other fine monuments of the period along the Thames Valley.

Long Wittenham already referred to as a later settlement taking its name from Little Wittenham, seems to have developed from a manor

Sir William Dunch & Family, d. 1611

and mill of Norman times, though this could have been preceded by a Saxon homestead of unknown name.

The river is bypassed for navigation by the Clifton Cut on the Oxfordshire side. The church of St. Mary the Virgin is at one end of this 'long' village, and near the manor site. Of the Norman church dated about 1100, there remains the west portion of the nave and the chancel arch with its square jambs and angle columns with decorative carving on the capitals.

Early English work is shown in the circular lead font which is almost identical with that at Warborough; there is another at Childrey in Berkshire. Here there are rosettes and wheels around the upper half above an arcade, each arch of which encloses a mitred figure. It stands on a massive stone base. In the 17th century the font was encased in wood and remained hidden until 1832. The cover is also of the 17th century, and is said, rather improbably, to have come from the canopy of the Jacobean pulpit in the 1850 alterations.

Between 1230 and 1250 the chancel was rebuilt and lengthened, and the south aisle and arcade with stiff-leaf capitals, was constructed. At the end of that century the south chapel, now the vestry, was built, probably by the widow of the crusader Gilbert de Clare, Earl of

Choir stall detail, Long Wittenham.

Gloucester and Hertford and lord of the manor, who died in 1295. His tomb recess is in the south wall, but there is a most remarkable monument in the form of the delightful piscina, in the same wall, which has angels hovering over the arch and, across the front edge, a tiny recumbent knight effigy.

The north aisle with its arcade was built about 1340. The very old south porch with its carved bargeboards and open side lights, may also date from then. Between 1425 and 1450 the west tower was added and early in the following century, the nave walls were raised – forming the clerestory – with a flatter roof. There was a major reconstruction in 1850 during which the chancel was rebuilt, but preserving most of the existing windows and other details, including a 13th century piscina. During work on the nave three pre-Reformation altar-slabs were found, further testifying to the multiplicity of altars in the medieval church.

In the chancel are the exceptionally fine 17th century choir stalls, with richly carved 'poppyheads', originally in Exeter College Chapel, Oxford, and brought here in 1875. The college has held the patronage of the church since 1322 and was responsible for the restorations.

To the north the river forms a great loop. The road runs close to the bank and, on turning past the justly famed Barley Mow Inn, crosses the Thames by an arched red-brick bridge to Clifton Hampden. Perched on a little eminence (the 'clif' of this hamlet) is the church of St. Michael and All Angels, its needle-like spirelet piercing the enclosing trees. The approach up winding steps on to a little terrace by the standing cross is truly romantic, as befits this lovely place.

From ancient times there was a ford here; a ferry plied until 1864 when the present bridge was built. As with Moulsford, the reason for the existence of a church and settlement seems closely tied to the crossing.

A chapel may well have existed in the Saxon period. During the 19th century a fragmentary carving was found in the vicinity of the porch, now located on the exterior of the north wall. This was attributed to about 1100 and leads to the conclusion that a stone church existed here after the Conquest. This crude piece of low-relief sculpture represents a boar hunt, the boar being on the left, and apparently being attacked about the ears by a dog; the man seemingly holding the dog's tail may, in fact, be holding a horn for any distinguishing detail is worn away. Originally it must have measured some five feet at least – rather large for a tympanum in a church of this size.

Other than this, the earliest identifiable architecture is the south arcade, with stone seat bases to two of the columns, of about 1180, indicating the addition of a south aisle to the nave at that time.

The north arcade dates from the mid 13th century; the aisle itself was enlarged in 1866.

Little else is known, other than that there was a lead font (presumably of similar date and pattern to those at Long Wittenham and Warborough), which was destroyed in the early 19th century.

130

Gargoyle, St. Michael's, Clifton Hampden.

Extensive restorations were begun under Sir G. G. Scott, 1843-4 continuing in 1866, and later. The patron for this work was the first Lord Aldenham whose father, George Henry Gibbs, is commemorated in effigy in the church. It is unfortunate that the church is gloomy inside and heavy with grossly elaborate chancel decorations and furnishings.

From Clifton Hampden one can follow the tow-pat past Clifton Lock and Cut towards Culham. The short stone spire of a church on the opposite bank signifies the presence of Appleford. As the name indicates this was once a fording place, and in the 15th and 16th centuries at least there was a bridge, witness contemporary references to a free chapel standing at the south end in 1511; now there is a 19th century railway viaduct.

It is very apparent that the church of Ss. Peter and Paul was heavily restored (indeed largely rebuilt and extended) in the mid 1880's. Prior to this there was a small church comprising nave and chancel, dating from the 12th and 13th centuries. In 1291 it is recorded as belonging to Abingdon Abbey; later it became a chapel of ease to Sutton Courtenay church. Inside, the octagonal font is also of the 13th century; the communion rails date from about 1730.

Westward along the river lies Sutton Courtenay. Just before the village one can cross to Culham on the north bank. By the 15th century there was a bridge, later damaged during the Civil War. After repair, it survived until the early 19th century when it was rebuilt.

Hereabouts, in the loop of the river, was Cula's meadow, Cul-hamm. The present village is an unhappy blend of old and new houses, the old being at the west end scattered around a green with a fine old manor house close to the church of St. Paul. The medieval building was rebuilt in the 'traditional' manner in the late 19th century, only retaining the very low west tower of 1710, with its decaying stucco-finish. Inside there is 17th century heraldic glass of the Cary family.

From Culham church there is a foot-path across the meadows, over the Cut and the thundering weirs of Sutton Pools, to the beautiful village of Sutton Courtenay. It is large, but spread out, so that there are new delights wherever one looks. From the 9th century the village is recorded as Suthtune, the southern homestead or village. Courtenay was the family name of the lords of the manor from Norman times. Before that there were pre-Roman and Romano-British settlements, as excavations have shown.

As a settled property it was given to the original Abbey of Abingdon in 687 A.D. It seems likely that there could have been a simple church here from such early days. Whatever building existed at the Conquest it may have proved adequate for a while, so that rebuilding only took place about 1150. The three lower stages of the tower and chancel arch responds belong to that time. The latter have carved capitals, to be compared with those at Long Wittenham. The responds were originally closer together and carrying a semi-circular arch; stones of the adjacent south arcade, with chevron and embattled decorating, could well be the remains of that arch, re-used.

The tower has clasping buttresses to the height of the first two storeys which are defined by string courses; the third storey terminates in a corbel table; above this is a rebuilt and heightened storey of the 14th century. The third stage is distinguished by three contemporary two-light windows with interlacing arches.

Less than a century after the Norman works, the chancel was rebuilt and extended eastwards. Alterations continued at relatively short intervals. There are three windows of the late 13th century; the west windows of both aisles and the east one of the north aisle. This suggests

132

re-use, for the arcades and aisles are of the 14th century. Much turns on dating which, without documentary evidence, is likely to be only a guide to within twenty years at best. In the building of the north arcade it may be that the nave was widened to the north, as the chancel and tower are off-centre.

The chancel arch was altered and widened at this time. In the following century the clerestory was formed, though there are older windows on the north side; these may have come from the aisles having been replaced by new, larger windows. The panelled south door may also date from this period, or from the early 16th century when the fine brick south porch was built with its parvise (room) above.

By 1901 the church was in urgent need of repair and an extensive but conservative restoration was carried out. During this work, two late 14th century table tombs were removed from the chancel, one providing an altar in the south aisle (where once was Brown's chantry chapel), the other being placed in the churchyard.

Further restoration took place from 1950-58, and in 1961 the north porch, built in 1850, was replaced with a vestry.

The spacious nave is favoured with many pleasing furnishings and notably the dominating font; it takes the typical tub form but ornamented with a deeply cut arcade enriched with fleur-de-lis, and dating from the late 12th century. It is topped with a simple 17th century oak cover. Also 17th century and of superior quality is the pulpit, which was given to the church in 1901.

The oak chancel screen, with its traceried arches, is the survivor of an early 15th century rood screen, but again not the rood in this church; this, and the choir stalls, were given in the 1880's. Indeed, the giving of old furnishings of distinction was a feature of the late 19th and early 20th centuries. The sources were in Europe or other churches in England which were discarding these fitments in pursuit of the newer liturgical and architectural ideals.

Apart from the altar tombs already referred to, the only other monument is an early 14th century tomb-recess in the chancel containing a rough stone effigy of a priest. The head, hands and feet were restored at the beginning of the century. Being very simple in its detail it is difficult to date; it could be contemporary with the tomb or later, possibly representing Reginald Mutt, d. 1500, first vicar of the church, who was buried before the high altar. The third possibility is that it was an early effigy which was recut, a known practice occurring also with fonts. Brasses were turned over and re-engraved, known as palimpsests, but this constituted a re-use of the material, rather than an alteration of the existing artefact.

Until the 1950-8 restoration, a medieval wall painting of St. George had survived, together with traces of a Doom painting over the chancel arch, parts of which must lie under the Royal Arms of Charles II, supported by the Commandments.

There are other paintings of the 17th century at the west end of the south wall, and over the tower arch a recent painting commemorating Edward Bradstock, founder of Appleford and Sutton schools, who died in 1607.

Abingdon Abbey, which had a grange nearby (known as the 'Abbey') was the patron until a dispute with the lord of the manor was resolved in 1284 in favour of the manor. By 1481, the advowson had passed to the dean and canons of St. George's, Windsor, in whose gift it remains.

The dedication of the church is to All Saints but, before the Reformation and certainly in the 15th century, it was to St. Mary the Virgin.

Due west and further from the river is the village of Drayton with its old street, and green at one end, and more recent suburban growth. The fine Georgian manor is worth noting. The church of St. Peter, with its four-square west tower stands out in the level landscape, which hems the narrow band of houses.

Documents show the existence of a village before the 10th century but no specific mention of a church till 1284. It is from about then, or slightly earlier, that the present building dates. This would accord with the new impetus in church building in the 13th century expressed in the early English style.

The plain Norman tub font is the only evidence remaining of an earlier church which must have existed from the late 11th century at least, probably as a very simple rectangular building. When rebuilt with chancel, nave and south chapel, it is possible that there was a balancing north chapel making a cruciform plan. This might account for the 13th century piscina in the north aisle which would have absorbed the north transept chapel when added in the 15th century. The west tower was also added at that time, and probably a south porch. The latter was extensively restored at the same time as the south chapel in the late 19th century. Earlier, in the mid 1850's, the chancel was rebuilt and fifteen years or so later further enlarged, with the addition of the vestry and organ chamber, 1871-2. In the vestry is a 15th century canopied niche, formerly in the north aisle.

Alabaster reredos, St. Peter's, Drayton.

In the south wall of the nave is a large 13th century piscina which has lost its head through the insertion of a later window above. It would probably have been similar to a recess at Little Marlow. Of the same date is the double-headed piscina in the south chapel, where there is also a later aumbry (cupboard) with wooden door.

Above the chapel altar is a remarkable survival of late 14th century carving in alabaster. This reredos, of six panels showing the Assumption, Annunciation, Adoration, Arrest, Scourging and Entombment was discovered buried in the churchyard in 1814. Representations of the Crucifixion and Resurrection are evidently missing if the theme is to be reasonably complete. These panels are most probably of English workmanship of the famous Nottingham school; similar ones exist at Yarnton, Oxfordshire. The quality of carving, once decorated, is very good; compare the Assumption with the later, coarser stone representation at Sandford-on-Thames and the Adoration with the decorated alabaster one at Hambleden. In the nave, close to the arch to the south chapel is a pleasing pulpit with carved panels of the early 17th century.

After leaving Drayton it is not long before a notable landmark

135

Interior, St. Peter's, Drayton.

draws one's attention; the spire of St. Helen's, Abingdon, punctuating the tranquil river plain. Whether approached over the fields, or along the river, or down the medieval streets around, it is a majestic sight. A spire was first erected in the late 15th century or early 16th century, being rebuilt in 1625 and again in 1888. The buttressed and pinnacled tower, which occupies an unusual north-east position, is older; it was built in the mid 13th century, together with the adjoining east wall of the outer north aisle, on the site of the Saxon church, the history of which probably began at the time the abbey was founded, 675 A.D. There is a specific documentary reference of about 995 A.D.

There is no fragment of Norman work whatsoever; either the subsequent rebuilding was very complete or the Saxon building was a substantial, albeit plain, one of stone which sufficed local needs until the mid 13th century. The abbey refounded in 995 A.D. dominated the town through those years, reaching its peak of prosperity under Abbot Fabritius between 1100 and 1117.

St. Helen's was appropriated to the abbey in 1261, and it was about

St. Helen's, Abingdon.

Roof painting, St. Helen's.

138

that date that William Reve founded the Lady Chapel at the east end of the inner north aisle. That aisle may well have been built at the same time, forming a south aisle to the original conjectural nave – the outer north aisle. From 1247 a Guild of Our Lady had been in existence supporting the church and probably instigated the reconstructions of the late 14th and 15th centuries.

The north wall had been altered, the south aisle widened, and the whole extended westward by 1391 when the splendid painted Lady Chapel roof was executed for William Cholsey. This was repaired in 1872-3, when decayed panels were removed, but not fully restored until 1933-5. There are alternating robed figures of prophets and kings standing on a vine forming a continuous link, a tree of Jesse.

The aisle of St. Helen, with its fine early Perpendicular arcades was also built about this time to serve as the main nave and chancel, which it is today.

The development was continued in 1420 by the Fraternity of the Holy Cross who had superseded the Guild. They commenced the aisle of St. Katherine, the present inner south aisle. The fraternity used to meet in the room over the north porch which they also built, together with the west porch. Between the north porch and the tower is a small two-storied building which once may have housed a priest or clerk.

By 1539 yet another aisle – the south, Holy Rood, or Reade aisle – was built with the south porch and vestry, making the church wider than it is long. In the vestry is an earlier piscina.

This multiplicity of aisles re-inforces the understanding of multiple usage in the medieval period. Thus the church was not used as a single volume as has been attempted for the past two centuries; the aisles were separate chapels with their own altars and priests and congregations, with frequent masses at differing times. Only on great festivals would one have found cohesion in concelebrated rites.

The church suffered much during the Civil War and Commonwealth periods. Later in 1706-7, galleries were inserted in the north and south aisles and box pews installed. In 1725 a west musician's gallery was added, together with a Jordan's organ, of which the fine case still survives. Further galleried seating was erected in the Lady aisle in 1796.

Then in 1872-3 extensive alteration was carried out under Woodyer, when the west wall was rebuilt, the nave heightened, the church re-pewed and the present screened chancel formed. The tall reredos partly concealing the east window was added in 1897 by Bodley.

Just inside the impressive main entrance, which passes under the

139

tower, stands the font, a 19th century copy of that at Sutton Courtenay. Here an upper vine band is shown which is probably a conjectural restoration for the top of the Sutton Courtenay font was probably cut away at an earlier date. The cover of 1634 once surmounted a wooden casing round an older, presumably Perpendicular, octagonal font. Just two years later is the handsome, restrained pulpit. Nearby is the imposing mayoral pew, reconstructed in 1706 with its carved lion and unicorn. In the centre of the nave hangs a marvellous brass chandelier of 1710; there are smaller examples in the aisles.

Two memorials vie for attention. Under a canopy are the tomb chest of John Roysse, d. 1571, who had founded the Grammar school eight years earlier and the marble tour-de-force of 1782 to Elizabeth Hawkins. There are many other memorials, and also two brasses of 1417 and 1501.

Leaving St. Helen's among its delightful almshouses by the river, and traversing the splendid diversity that is East St. Helen's Street, one reaches the square which is dominated by the grand 17th century County Hall by Christopher Kempster.

Just across the square is the well-restored 15th century gateway to the once great abbey, now a few scattered ruins. Forming the north side of that entrance is the church of St. Nicolas which was built as a chapel for the abbey servants and for visitors about 1180. It then consisted of a small nave and chancel, probably extending not much further east than the present chancel arch. The west end has its original though restored, late Norman arcading and doorway; there are the remains of a typical clasping buttress at the south-west angle.

In the rioting of 1327 the south wall was pulled down and had to be rebuilt. The chancel may well have been rebuilt by then or soon after, but as it stands today it is of the 15th century when the west tower was erected actually within the west end of the nave. Presumably this was because the church's very limited site allowed no other possibility. The south porch also belongs to that period, and possibly the tiny chapel off the nave to the north, though this has been credited to the 1881 restoration when much work was done.

Other examples of the 15th century are the pleasing octagonal font, and in the vestry, a fragment of a stone reredos showing the Crucifixion with St. Mary, St. John and St. Nicolas.

The carved and panelled oak pulpit is of a similar age to that at St. Helen's; here the desk is supported by two eagles.

In 1881 the tall colourful monument to John Blacknall, d. 1625, with

St. Nicolas, Abingdon.

141

its altar tomb, plain reredos and kneeling figures above within an architectural framework, was moved into the small north chapel. Restoration was necessary following a fire in 1953; exterior cleaning has been carried out very recently.

The site is very unusual in that the church is actually built over a stream, the Stert; one reason that could be advanced is that this stream at the entrance to the abbey had long been a place of baptism.

In a newer part of Abingdon – Northcourt – Christ Church was founded in 1961 utilising a stone tithe barn, once belonging to the abbey.

Although there are many traces of early settlement around the town, Abingdon would seem to have begun as a Saxon noblewoman's hill settlement, Aebbe's dun; an early documented name is Abendon which persisted till the 16th century. It is suggested that the site was away from the river, but was moved perhaps following the foundation of the first abbey in 675 A.D.

After the demise of that abbey, an important meeting took place there in 926 A.D. between King Athelstan and his council, and a mission from Hugh, Duke of the Franks. Athelstan was offered perfumes, gems, horses, an onyx vase, a diadem set with jewels, and notably a number of fabulous relics comprising the sword of Constantine the Great with a nail from the Cross set in its hilt; the lance of Charlemagne which had pierced the Lord's side; the standard of St. Maurice the martyr; and fragments of the Cross and Crown of Thorns set in crystal.

About 980 A.D. another meeting, a king's great council, was held at Abingdon.

The crossing of the river Thames was not good in the early days for a boat had to be used to cross the main stream, followed by a marshy trek across Andersey and then fording the backwater. This was overcome by a bridge and causeway, but still leaving a ferry across the river. At the instigation of the town's merchants, permission was obtained to build a bridge and this was completed in 1416; it became the major crossing point in the area to the detriment of Wallingford.

CHAPTER XI

Abingdon to Oxford

In 1284 when John de Clifford, the nominee of Abingdon Abbey, was instituted as Vicar of St. Helen's his income included the oblations and lesser tithes of the chapel of Radley, except the tithes of lambs, wool and cheese.

That chapel, now the church of St. James the Great, stands some two miles to the north-east of the town, not at the present centre of population but with little more than school and farm at hand. But it is also on the edge of Radley Park and College, probably the site of a Saxon manor which passed into the possession of Abingdon Abbey before Domesday, as did the lands for many miles around.

A Norman chapel is known to have existed, comprised in all probability of nave and chancel only. The unexpectedly elaborate font is late Norman work, c. 1180, with an arcaded cylinder supported on four short columns, each different in its decorative detail. In 1840 it was discovered in the farm nearby and 'restored'.

About the end of the 13th century there was a major rebuilding resulting it would seem in a church with nave, chancel and north and south transept chapels. Extensive alterations were made in the second half of the 15th century, with the addition of aisles with unusual high oak-pillared arcades, the small west tower, and all the windows, except in the south transept.

In 1643 a skirmish in the Civil War caused the destruction of the north aisle and transept, which were not rebuilt. Ten years later William Lenthall, speaker of the House of Commons, who had married into the local Stonhouse family, gave the fine oak pulpit canopy – late Perpendicular work – said to be from over his chair in the Commons. The present pulpit belongs to the 18th century.

The imposing carved and traceried choir stalls with high backs and cherub's head misericords are from Cologne, c. 1600, brought here by Sir George Bowyer in 1847.

Sir William Stonhouse d. 1631, Radley.

144

Choir Stalls c. 1600, St. James', Radley.

Other alterations and restorations took place in the 19th century including the addition of the south porch in 1877. There was a major restoration in 1902.

Dominating the sanctuary, to the south of the altar, is a large finely detailed and executed marble and alabaster monument, partly decorated, by Nicholas Stone to commemorate Sir William Stonhouse, d. 1631, and his son John, d. 1632. Sir William and his wife lie recumbent with the son kneeling on the right; in front of the base are figures of two sons, five daughters and four chrysom children.

The particular treasure of this church is the glowing abundance of stained glass with its marvellous colourings. This is said to be of French or Flemish manufacture of the 16th century, presumably for an English client for most of the glass portrays coats of arms of the English sovereigns including Richard III, Henry VI, Henry VII and Henry VIII.

Beyond the new and expanding village by the railway to the east, is the old village on the level river plain where early man settled. Across the river are the wooded slopes of Nuneham Park and the great 18th century mansion. The private chapel there was built by the first Earl Harcourt who demolished the medieval church which stood nearer the A423 trunk road. Yet another church, to serve the villagers of Nuneham Courtenay, was built in 1860; this is now closed.

A short distance the other side of the trunk road, down a tree-screened lane, stands St. Peter's church, close to Basildon House and a little apart from the rest of the village.

Marsh Baldon – probably the marshy area by Bealda's hill at Toot Baldon – was a Saxon settlement, straddling the Roman road from Dorchester to Alcester.

Recorded mention of a church does not occur till 1163. However, a Saxon chapel very probably existed, served perhaps from Dorchester Abbey. Reset over the south doorway, under an old porch, is a circular mass-dial with a cable-roll surround; it is so simple that it could be either late Saxon or early Norman. Equally inconclusive is the rough voussoired semi-circular arch immediately above. The doorway below is a later insertion.

In 1341 the church, comprising nave and chancel, was extensively altered and extended, with the addition of the west tower which has an uncomfortably odd octagonal upper storey, perhaps intended to carry a spire.

Further alterations were made during the 15th century including the piscina in the sanctuary. A major restoration took place in 1880, when the north aisle was added.

The interior is favoured with a good carved oak pulpit, still with tester and backboard, dating from 1662. On the south wall is a distinguished rococo style monument of the mid 18th century. Glowing over all is the fine collection of stained glass in the east window; most is from the 14th century including the central figure of St. Anne with her daughter, the Blessed Virgin Mary, and on either side, the sad figures of Mary again and St. John. Originally these two would have stood either side of a central Crucifixion panel. Below are heraldic arms from the 16th century; there are more of these in the south chancel window.

The main road northward brings one closer to the river again and to Sandford-on-Thames, now bypassed. This rather plain village extends thinly past the church to the lock and mill. Its origins lie in its name, a sandy ford, of localised importance for no crossing has survived. A manor, and perhaps a mill, stood hereabouts in Saxon times.

In the late 13th century the manor was granted to the Knights Templars for a preceptory which seems to have been at the old farmhouse between the church and river. After the Conquest the estate passed to Jerrie de Planastre who built St. Andrew's church before 1100. In the level country around it presents a substantial and crisp appearance with its 'roofless' tower and heavily restored stonework, all exposed rubble, only softened by the expansive shade of a yew. Particularly striking is the very tall late 12th century belfry window in the low two-storied tower; other windows were inserted in the church at that time. The original east and south walls remain with the plain south and north doorways, the latter blocked and out of position because of the north aisle which was added in 1863.

Apart from further changes to windows and other details, the basic building remained much the same until the 19th century, except for the quaint stone porch built in 1652 during the Commonwealth when churches were closed and worship forbidden.

Inside, the great treasure is on the south wall of the chancel: it is a large carved stone panel of the late 15th century showing the Assumption of the Blessed Virgin Mary. Three angels attend her on each side and, at her feet, two more hold a reliquary. These angels are similar in detail to those in the chancel of St. Peter's, Caversham. It is of average quality and in good condition having escaped the iconoclasts, apparently by being buried, for it was dug up from below the porch floor in 1724.

Carving of the Virgin, Sandford.

The main road quickly plunges into suburban Oxford of which Iffley is but part. But Iffley down leafy lanes to the river and lock is a beautiful world apart. The Saxons saw here a wood, the haunt of plovers, so naming it Gifetelea, the earliest documented form in 1004.

A Saxon church could have existed and it has been suggested that there was one of stone. However, between 1175 and 1182, Robert de St. Remi, lord of the manor, erected one of the most perfect small churches of his time to St. Mary the Virgin and it has only been altered in one major respect with the complementary addition of the lovely chancel in the early English style, perhaps some sixty years later. Apart from this then, and the insertion of 14th and 15th century windows, the whole structure, with its very varied but controlled enrichment, is a splendid example of the Anglo-Norman style at its culmination.

The central tower, with its good ashlar stonework in the upper storey, and external stair with its rare ribbed turret, is the same width as the nave and choir. As the latter would have served as the original chancel, perhaps with a small eastern apse, the significance of the central tower is obscure unless there were transepts, or the concept was largely a matter of fashion in imitation of the major churches and cathedrals of the period. The tower arches are richly carved and shafted, including octagonal shafts of slate. The choir is vaulted with great ribs of chevron pattern; also vaulted is the later chancel in its own imcomparably delicate manner. A complementary group of aumbry, piscina and sedilia is in the south wall.

At the west end is the vast square font, its black stone bowl supported on a squat centre column with three spiral-fluted corner columns and one odd one. The whole has been much patched and restored indicating that it was probably discarded at some time, perhaps for the octagonal font bowl now weathering away outside the west door.

The magnificent west front has three lights in the gable, a restored round window below, and a great west doorway flanked by two blind arches. Of the doorway's many decorative elements the beakheads are particularly fine. The outer band has very varied carvings including signs of the zodiac.

By comparison the north doorway to the nave is plain, but the south doorway is equally splendid, especially as its carvings were protected by a porch until 1807. The many vigorous scenes include knights on horseback, centaurs with one suckling its young, and a man fighting a dragon-like animal. Further to the east of this doorway, probably alongside the chancel, an anchoress, Annora, had a cell about 1240.

149

St. Mary's, Iffley.
150

In the 1820's earlier furnishings were removed. The nave roof was raised to its original pitch in 1844, fourteen years later the round west window was restored and in 1864 the sanctuary arcading was inserted. The organ, installed in 1875, replaced an 18th century west singers' gallery. In 1907 the pulpit was made to the design of Sir Ninian Comper. Further restoration work has been carried out in recent years and as with all churches is a continuing pattern of both conservation and alteration.

Across the Thames and the Hinksey Stream, which joins the Thames only a little way downstream, is South Hinksey, still a village despite the imminence of Oxford. It was just Hinksey – North and South conjoined – in early times. The place-name Hengestesige indicates most probably that stallions were kept on an island; less likely is its derivation from Hengist, the Saxon founder of Kent. By 1316 South Hinksey had a separate identity, and a small stone chapel, perhaps a century old. It is interesting that the dedication to St. Laurence should be repeated at North Hinksey which was probably the main settlement with the older and more important place of worship.

Today South Hinksey church still has its early 13th century nave; the west tower may have been added later that century, but most of its features are now of the 15th century. The chancel was largely rebuilt in the 18th century.

Remains of stairs near the narrow chancel arch indicate the former existence of a rood beam. Now there is a screen, supporting a rood, erected in 1932. The pulpit and prayer desk, of 1936, are fine examples of recent craftsmanship.

Much older work is that of the very small, rather battered, double piscina, barely twelve inches high with a triple arched head, situated in the south wall of the nave and possibly contemporary with it.

Between the Hinkseys and Oxford lies a network of streams and rivers; the crossing was important because this whole length of the middle and upper Thames was a much disputed area between the Saxon kingdoms of Wessex and Mercia. Oxnaford (Oxenford) was its early name which became that of the city, a comparatively late foundation among cities. Several religious institutions were established here, notably St. Frideswide's 8th century priory on the site of Christ Church. In the late 9th and early 10th centuries it was being fortified against the Danish raiders; this measure of security led to the growth of a town first mentioned in 912 A.D. By 925 A.D. there was a mint. Nevertheless Oxford was burnt in 1010 and captured in 1013. Danish rule was consolidated under King Cnut who held a national assemble here in 1018.

By then the tower of St. Michael's church, at the north gate of the old city, was probably in existence. Exactly how the church related to the defences and gateway is not known. The rugged seventy feet high tower, the oldest building in Oxford, may have served as a lookout, the bells being used for alarm as well as calling to worship. It is of rubble construction, probably rendered over originally, with typical long and short quoining on the northern angles, but rubble quoining on the south. Massive iron strapping has been applied to re-inforce the weakening structure. There are seven upper windows, double-headed with supporting centre balusters set halfway through the wall thickness. Midway up the north face is a tall opening of unknown purpose. At the base is a blocked west doorway formed with monolithic quoins. In the 15th century the east tower arch was formed. A cupola was added to the top in the late 17th century but taken down in 1700 as being dangerous. By 1832 the tower was in danger of being demolished because of its poor condition. Repair work was eventually carried out in 1852. and in 1853-4 there was a major restoration of the whole church under G. E. Street. In 1873 the plain parapet was built in place of a battlement top of 1500. Two years later some of the old windows were re-opened, having been blocked up for centuries. Further work was necessary in 1896; again in 1908 when the tower was buttressed at the north-east and south-east angles, and in 1957.

In the rest of the church all early work has disappeared, but the narrow nave may well be the plan of the Saxon one. The chancel was rebuilt in the early 13th century; the arch, lancet windows and piscina all remain, having been re-used during the 19th century rebuilding.

The Lady Chapel, to the north of the chancel, may have been founded in the 13th century as well, though no work earlier than the 14th century remains. A mid 13th century chapel is also said to have existed on the site of the north transept, rebuilt in 1833. About 1280 a south chapel at the east of the south aisle was added, possibly dedicated to St. Thomas of Canterbury. To the west of this was added another in 1342, perhaps to St. Katherine.

In the late 15th century the north aisle was built; the arcades were formed as they are today; the south porch was erected with its pleasing stone-vaulted roof and re-using a 13th century archway; the sedilia were formed; the much restored pulpit was installed; a font, now at Yarnton in Oxfordshire, was provided; four image niches were inserted and a rood screen was installed, which survived until the 1853-4 restoration when the 18th century box pews, chandeliers and west

St. Michael's, Northgate, Oxford.

153

gallery were also removed.

In 1932 a new altar arrangement was provided in place of G. E. Street's reredos. The Lady Chapel was restored, 1939-41, following the removal of the organ. The later organ of 1947, together with the roofs, was destroyed by fire in 1953. As a result of this the choir was repositioned with a new organ, and a choir vestry was added.

Amidst all these changes, that most fragile of artefacts, stained glass, has survived from as early as 1290. This is in the east window and comprises four well drawn figures representing the Virgin and Child, St. Michael and the dragon, a bishop, possibly St. Nicholas, and St. Edmund of Abingdon, Archbishop of Canterbury, 1234-45. In a north aisle window are some late 15th century fragments, including the rare central representation of Christ crucified on a lily. There are a number of minor wall monuments, and two late brasses.

In the Domesday survey, four churches are recorded for Oxford, including St. Michael's, but other chapels also must have existed, and all these multiplied as the medieval period advanced. Another church of early foundation, revealing extensive Norman work including a crypt, is St. Peter's-in-the-East, now a library for St. Edmund Hall.

Of traditionally early origin is the great university church of St. Mary the Virgin in the High, for a 9th century church is said to have stood on the site. Considering the rapid development of Oxford this is quite probable and if destroyed in 1010 when the Danes burnt the town, it may well have been rebuilt and be the church referred to in Domesday. It is believed that it was rebuilt again between 1150 and 1200, in the late Norman manner.

Of these buildings there are no indications; the earliest part of today's church is the massive tower begun about 1280 and completed by 1320 with its superb soaring spire. This tower occupies an unusual north position and would have been extended from the 12th century church if, as has been suggested, it consisted of nave and chancel in similar positions to the present. A number of possibilities might be considered. The 11th or 12th century church could have been cruciform in plan with transepts where the eastern ends of the aisles now are, and with a central tower. As was quite common, it might have been necessary to demolish the central tower and rebuild elsewhere. The normal position would be at the west, but a site limitation could have prevented this; the secondary sites would then be to the north or south of the transepts. Or, the present tower might be on the site of an 11th century tower, itself the centre of a cruciform

154

St. Mary's, Oxford.

155

church. The limitations on expansion imposed by such a central tower could have led to the building of a larger nave and chancel alongside. In both hypotheses subsequent rebuilding would obliterate the stages of development, as did in fact happen. The identified site of St. Catherine's chapel, one of five in the 12th century church, could be accounted for in each case as a transeptal chapel.

Following the completion of the spire, the Old Congregation House was built to the east of the tower, 1320-7, to provide the university with its first building. This has two storeys, the lower with its vaulted roof used as a crypt chapel.

To the west of the tower, in 1328, Adam de Brome, founder of Oriel College, built the Lady Chapel, and there stands his tomb. He was the last rector for he appropriated the rectorial rights to his college which has appointed the vicars ever since.

This close association led to the rebuilding of the chancel in 1462 by Walter Lyhert, Bishop of Norwich, and formerly Provost of Oriel. It is a wonderfully dignified place with its great clear windows, canopied eastern niches (restored with modern figures), rich sedilia and piscina, and fine contemporary oak stalls and panelling. The reredos and rails belong to the late 17th restorations.

To complement this work, the nave and aisles were completely rebuilt between 1490 and 1503, resulting in the spacious and graceful interior and completing the church one admires today, except for the highly individual baroque south portico erected in 1637 to the design of Nicholas Stone.

In 1827 there was a complete refitting of the interior with pews and galleries, and the present pulpit and font. The galleries were removed later that century and other changes made in conformity with changing liturgical requirements. Restoration work was carried out as well, notably in 1893 when the spire was repaired involving the replacement of all but one of its statues.

A fire in 1946 brought further renovations, and the building of a new organ; some 17th century casework was preserved and re-used.

There are numerous monuments, many of considerable historical interest including those to Amy Robsart, d. 1560; and Dr. Radcliffe, d. 1714, after whom the Radcliffe Camera and Infirmary are named. In the tower is a brass to Edmund Croston, principal of Brasenose Hall, who died in 1508; two bands of carved stone, above and below, are said to have belonged to the great early 16th century pulpit, destroyed in the Commonwealth period.

What is not recorded in stone and wood and metal, is that in this

156

Brass c. 1584, St. Mary's.

157

lovely place Archbishop Cranmer and Bishops Ridley and Latimer were tried and condemned to death by burning.

There are many other churches of interest and importance in Oxford, but the two described suffice to illustrate the early history and different development of parish churches in this place.

The Thames Valley, as we have seen, is rich in historic architecture both religious and secular, a great heritage from the past. The first step to preserving this heritage, is to learn about it, for to know it, in time, means to love it.

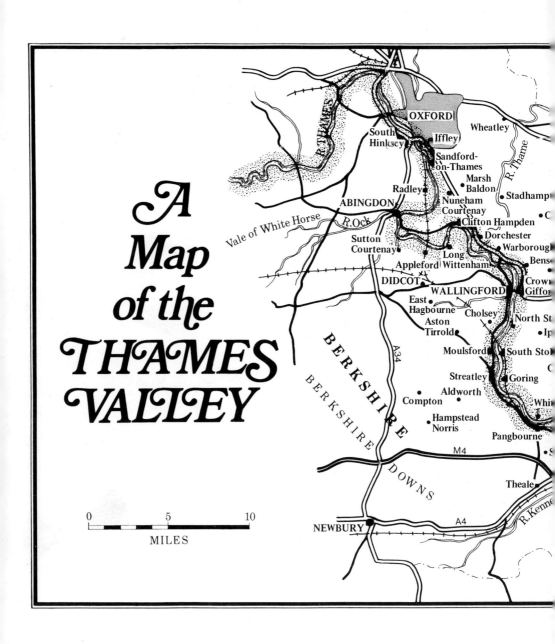

A Map of the THAMES VALLEY

OXFORD

Wheatley

South Hinksey

Iffley

R. THAMES

R. Thame

Sandford-on-Thames

Marsh Baldon

Stadhamp

Radley

Nuneham Courtenay

ABINGDON

Clifton Hampden

Vale of White Horse

R. Ock

Dorchester

Warborough

Sutton Courtenay

Long Wittenham

Bens

Appleford

Crow Giffor

DIDCOT

WALLINGFORD

East Hagbourne

Cholsey

North St

Aston Tirrold

Ip

Moulsford

South Sto

BERKSHIRE

A34

Streatley

Goring

BERKSHIRE

Aldworth

Compton

Whi

Hampstead Norris

Pangbourne

BERKSHIRE DOWNS

M4

Theale

NEWBURY

A4

R. Kenne

0   5   10

MILES